Yoruba Oral Tradition in Islamic Nigeria

I0129091

This book traces Dàdàkúàdá's history and artistic vision and discusses its vibrancy as the most popular traditional Yoruba oral art form in Islamic Africa.

Foregrounding the role of Dàdàkúàdá in Ilorin, and of Ilorin in Dàdàkúàdá, this book covers the history, cultural identity, performance techniques, language, social life, and relationship with Islam of the oral genre. The author examines Dàdàkúàdá's relationship with Islam and discusses how the Dàdàkúàdá singers, through their songs and performances, are able to accommodate Islam in ways that have ensured their continued survival as a traditional African genre in a predominantly Muslim community.

This book will be of interest to scholars of traditional African culture, African art history, performance studies, and Islam in Africa.

Abdul-Rasheed Na'Allah is Professor of English and Comparative Poetics and Vice-Chancellor of Kwara State University, Malete, Nigeria. He is the coauthor of *Introduction to African Oral Literature and Performance* (2005), and the author of *Africanity, Islamicity and Performativity* (2009), *African Discourse in Islam, Oral Traditions, and Performance* (2010), *Cultural Globalization And Plurality* (2011), and *Globalization, Oral Performance and African Traditional Poetry* (2018).

Global Africa
Series Editors: Toyin Falola and Roy Doron

Yoruba Oral Tradition in Islamic Nigeria
A History of Dàdàkúàdá

Abdul-Rasheed Na'Allah

R Routledge
Taylor & Francis Group

LONDON AND NEW YORK

First published 2020
by Routledge
2 Park Square, Milton Park, Abingdon, Oxon OX14 4RN

and by Routledge
605 Third Avenue, New York, NY 10017

First issued in paperback 2021

Routledge is an imprint of the Taylor & Francis Group, an informa business

© 2020 Abdul-Rasheed Na'Allah

The right of Abdul-Rasheed Na'Allah to be identified as author of
this work has been asserted by him in accordance with sections 77
and 78 of the Copyright, Designs and Patents Act 1988.

All rights reserved. No part of this book may be reprinted or
reproduced or utilised in any form or by any electronic, mechanical,
or other means, now known or hereafter invented, including
photocopying and recording, or in any information storage or
retrieval system, without permission in writing from the publishers.

Trademark notice: Product or corporate names may be trademarks
or registered trademarks, and are used only for identification and
explanation without intent to infringe.

British Library Cataloguing-in-Publication Data
A catalogue record for this book is available from the British Library

Library of Congress Cataloging-in-Publication Data
Names: Na'Allah, Abdul Rasheed, author.
Title: Yoruba oral tradition in Islamic Nigeria: a history of Dàdàkúàdá /
Abdul-Rasheed Na'Allah.
Description: New York: Routledge, 2019. | Series: Global Africa; 14 |
Includes bibliographical references and index.
Identifiers: LCCN 2019016159 (print) | LCCN 2019016700 (ebook) |
ISBN 9780429295164 (ebook) | ISBN 9781000186543 (Adobe Reader) |
ISBN 9781000207262 (Mobipocket) | ISBN 9781000227987 (ePub3) |
ISBN 9780367260323 (hardback)
Subjects: LCSH: Folk songs, Yoruba—Nigeria—Ilorin. | Folk songs,
Yoruba—History and criticism. | Folk songs, Yoruba—Religious
aspects—Islam. | Oral tradition—Nigeria—Ilorin.
Classification: LCC PL8823.5 (ebook) | LCC PL8823.5 .N36 2019 (print) |
DDC 896.3331—dc23
LC record available at https://lccn.loc.gov/2019016159

ISBN 13: 978-0-367-78795-0 (pbk)
ISBN 13: 978-0-367-26032-3 (hbk)

Typeset in Times New Roman
by codeMantra

For:
My dearest father, Ahmad Alabi Na'Allah, whose love for knowledge and faith in God have been my inspirations; for the loving memory of my paternal grandmother, Saratu Iyapopo Odee Aro, Odee Ogo lalagbede, Ode Ogo nile Akaje; and for Jaigbade Alao and all other Dàdàkúàdá artists, dead or living.

Contents

Preface

In writing this book, I have taken the premise that a performing art of a people would be better understood and appreciated from a background knowledge into those people's history and their cultural and economic lives. I have also invoked the principle of participatory performance, which basically insists that a more authentic interpretation of a performance life would derive from a direct experience from and participation in the actual performance (see Na'Allah, 1997; Na'Allah and Ogunjimi, 2005). Having been born in Ilorin and lived there for many years, I was privileged to live a life of Dàdàkúàdá audience, in which I attended performances; patronized Dàdàkúàdá artists when they performed during naming and wedding ceremonies and constantly listened to their songs on radio, gramophone records, and cassette tape players; and saw them on television programs at home and outside home.

In 1985, I started what seems now a lifetime of fieldwork into Dàdàkúàdá history and performance techniques, attending performances, visiting Dàdàkúàdá artists at home, interviewing them, and occasionally participating in performances. I wrote my B.A. (Hons) English and Education Degree Long Essay on "Dàdàkúàdá: Trends in the Development of an Ilorin Oral Art" (1988). Living in Canada and the United States between 1994 and 2009, I continued to listen to and perform Dàdàkúàdá songs into the twenty-first century. As the convener of the 34th Annual Conference of African Literature Association in 2008, I invited the King of Dàdàkúàdá performers to the United States and selected a stage for Dàdàkúàdá performance on a US University campus. At home in Ilorin and Malete from 2009 to 2019, I invited Dàdàkúàdá artists to campus of Kwara State University, to perform regularly to staff and students, providing platform for Dàdàkúàdá artists in the University. In scholarly arena to friends and colleagues around the world, Dàdàkúàdá is among important art forms that have helped me and in many cases my family in performing our Ilorinness.

Following in the footsteps of Dandatti AbdulKadir and relying on his seminal work on Mamam Shata Katsina, I provide in this book a basis for comparative study by starting my discussions with a "brief trip" into the early study of oral poetry of the Homer and of some parts of Africa. Although not many studies have taken up the challenge to inquire or problematize the Homeric study, it is interesting that many theoretical insights of scholars of Homeric songs are easily identifiable even in the twenty-first-century studies of oral performance in Africa. More than anything else, the twentieth-century assertion of currency and contemporaneity in oral traditions remain strong even in the twenty-first century. Scholars have continued to explore oral performances on cyberspace and to demonstrate that orality can adequately reflect contemporary daily life situations and satisfy aesthetic yearnings of people in older communities as well as in New World nations.[1]

This book briefly reviews the form and characteristics of many Ilorin traditional poetic genres and presents the origin and the developmental stages of Dàdàkúàdá. I have used several names for the Dàdàkúàdá performer: poet, singer, artist, performer, all intended to adequately represent how they see themselves and what their community calls them. Comparing Dàdàkúàdá poetry with other numerous oral art forms of Ilorin, I identify Dàdàkúàdá as relatively more popular than the other oral poetry genres in the category of modern-day secular poetry in Ilorin. Also, this work examines the influence of Islam on Dàdàkúàdá performances and on its performance themes as since 1820s Ilorin has attained a status as a Muslim city. The different characteristics of a Dàdàkúàdá field performance, including the roles of every member of a Dàdàkúàdá performance group, are presented.

Language is a crucial element of Dàdàkúàdá as it is with any poetry. To appreciate the Dàdàkúàdá language, one may need to understand the poet's word choice and other language uses in Dàdàkúàdá, and this book attempts to take readers through this experience in analyzing the language of Dàdàkúàdá. I also discuss the influence of Hausa and other linguistic forms on the language of Dàdàkúàdá. Instrumentation is another key element of Dàdàkúàdá performance. I look at functions of drum language in the performance.

Apprenticeship is a very important system in African traditional oral art. It is through apprenticeship that new generations of professionals were, and would continue to be, ensured. I briefly address the steps undergone by an apprentice to Dàdàkúàdá. I examine, as an example of Dàdàkúàdá's contemporaneity, the themes of partisanship

and politics in Dàdàkúàdá, using Odolaye Aremu who has been identified as the most partisan of Dàdàkúàdá artists. This book also examines other aspects of political, moral, and didactic dimensions of
Dàdàkúàdá.
In the conclusion, this book takes another look at the performance
patterns and characteristics of Dàdàkúàdá, in light of some important
performance theories as well as the unique historicity of Dàdàkúàdá
and the influence of its development traditions on it.

Note

1 Abiola Irele, together with another scholar, provides praise poetry of a
   South African ethnic group on cyberspace for interested scholars and re-
   searchers. And, Mshai Mwangola, in her paper, "Transcending Boundaries: Performing the Contemporary African Diaspora" discusses the use
   of orature on cyberspace by an immigrant who tries to "make home after
   leaving home."

Acknowledgments

I owe a great deal of gratitude to the Almighty Allah and to many people across nations (Nigeria, Canada, the United States, and more) for the successful completion of this manuscript. This book is a lifetime study starting from my childhood and became formalized during my undergraduate days from the early to the late 1980s. My unending gratitude to Allah Subhanahu wa ta'ala, for guiding me through this undertaking. I am grateful to Dr. (Rev.) Gabriel Ajadi, together with the late Bayo Ogunjimi, who laid a solid scholarly foundation for my interest in researching and writing about African oral tradition. Ajadi encouraged every stage of my research on Dàdàkúàdá during my study at the University of Ilorin and offered erudite advice. I also thank Professor Oludare Olajubu, former Dean of Arts, University of Ilorin, and Professor Olu Obafemi, for showing a great interest in my work and helping me at every stage. Olajubu and I paid a visit to Odolaye Aremu in his Ilorin family house. Professor Olajubu's exceptionally brilliant M.A. Thesis on *Iwi*, a Yoruba oral poetry, was equally greatly helpful. I got important insights from the writings of Dandatti AbdulKadir on the poetry of Mamman Shata Katsina, the late doyen of African performance poetry. Between 1986 and 2018, I became quite close to many Dàdàkúàdá poets, with most recent visits to their family houses in May 2008 to update some of my materials and a short interview with Jaigbade Alao in 2011 to prepare a short proposal for submission to a committee in Abuja for a possible consideration of a Nigerian National Award for him. Since this book is about oral art history, I have equally relied on materials I collected in 1987 as well as the new ones I collected in 2008. I count myself lucky though I had a unique opportunity to personally interact with all the twentieth-century legends of Dàdàkúàdá. I interviewed them, attended their public performances, and got close to their immediate families: I am forever grateful to Jaigbade Alao, Omoekee Amao, Odolaye Aremu, Aremu

Ose, Saka Kolobo, and others for their kindness and generosity! Unfortunately, four of these legends have now died, thus underscoring the urgency for this work. Omoekee Amao (died around 1987), Odolaye Aremu (around 1997), Aremu Ose (close to the end of 2007), and Saka Kolobo, more recently. I hope this book will serve their great memory.

My unending gratitude goes to all friends, in Ilorin, Nigeria, and abroad, who were tremendously helpful: Sa'adu Imam Agbaji, AbdulRasaq Abdullahi Eleyinla, Hameed Dare Abdul, Abubakar Al-Imam Aligan, Ramat Abdullahi (Ambursa), Imam AbdulQadir, and Taofeeq Niyi Tijani. I remain grateful to my loving father, the late Ahmed Na'Allah, and my dearest mother, Bilkis Olohuntoyin Na'Allah, for their financial and moral support during my initial fieldwork. I also thank my aunt, Alhaja Ayinke Azeez Afunku; my eldest sisters, Maryam AbdulWahab Elelu and Mojirayo Giwa; my brothers, AbdulRasaq AbdulKareem and Abdullahi Na'Allah; and all other members of my extended family for their various contributions. I thank my immediate family, starting from my *Karamah*, to all the children. I am very grateful to Alhaji J.A. Fatayi who was the first person to type my original manuscript in Ilorin on cyclostyle papers and to Sherry Brown, who later retyped it in Chicago and saved it on a Microsoft Word file. I thank Erica Potterbaum for proofreading it and offering very useful suggestions. I also thank all other readers for their insights and enthusiasms.

Finally, let me return again to the poets, I thank Alhaji Jaigbade Alao, Aremu Ose, Omoekee Amao, Odolaye Aremu, and other Dàdàkúàdá artists for their cooperation during my fieldwork.

Malete, Kwara State, 2018

1 Geography and culture of Ilorin

Although politically situated as part of Northern Nigeria (North Central), Ilorin is popularly known to Nigerians as "the gateway town between the Northern and the Southern parts of Nigeria." Anyone crossing to the north from the southwest may often pass through Ilorin and vice versa. Ilorin is just about 100 km away from Oyo and 40 km from Ogbomoso (both cities in the southwest), on latitude North 8°30' and longitude East 4°35',[1] and occupies savannah grassland, which forms its vegetation.[2]

Ilorin town is not synonymous with Ilorin land. Ilorin land includes many villages and hamlets, some as far away from Ilorin town as 80 km. Among Ilorin people, the phenomenon of Ilorin town and Ilorin land is often described as *Ile Ilorin* and *Oko Ilorin*, literally "the Ilorin house/home" and "the Ilorin suburb/village," and the two concepts feature constantly in spiritual, economic, and political dialogues of Ilorin people. It is common to hear these terms used in every mosque in Ilorin, as most leaders pray for both *Ile Ilorin* and *Oko Ilorin*. It is often said that there is no Ilorin person that claims an origin at home without a root at the village or the suburb or vice versa! Yet these are the two concepts that can only be understood from the multicultural identity tradition of Ilorin. Ilorin land is, in the twenty-first century, synonymous with Ilorin Emirate, which now spreads across several local government areas (e.g. Asa, Moro, Ilorin West, Ilorin East local government areas).[3] Here are maps that perhaps show the Emirate clearly (Figure 1.1).[4]

These maps show that Ilorin Emirate covered and still covers many communities, cities, and villages, and easily presents an important opportunity for the oral performer to seek patrons from the entire emirate as indigene of the emirate. Yet, not all parts of the Ilorin Emirate of the 1920s share the same cultural, social, and religious identities as Ilorin city.

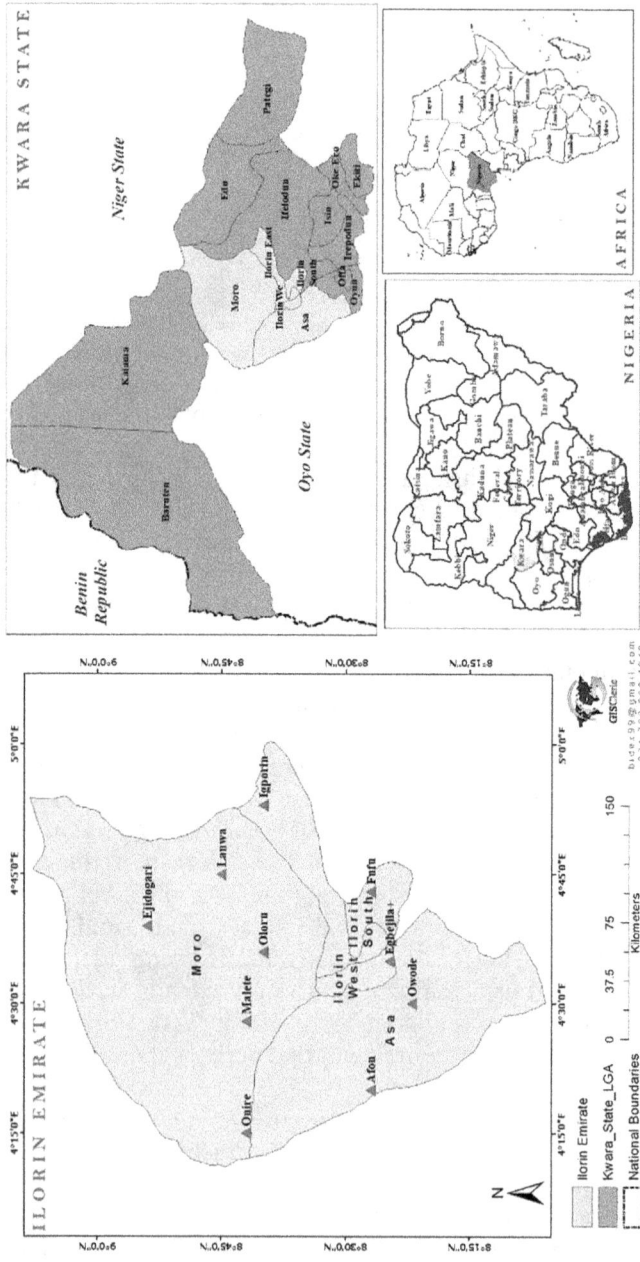

Figure 1.1 Maps showing Ilorin Emirate.

In the twenty-first century, Ilorin city is not just an urban city in the true sense of an African urban city of the global age but a city unique for being truly African traditional in terms of its cultural features, and at the same time being modern and globalized, in the full sense of a twenty-first century global city. The Ilorin villages and suburbs are rubbed off from these characteristics to some extent, yet they are principally heavily conservative culturally, far more than Ilorin city. Ilorin culture is rooted in the history of ethnic amalgamation and pluralities. Here is a poem that may help explain Ilorin roots and origins:

Ilorin Afonja

Ilo irin, Ilorin
Iron sharpener, for the hunters,
That's what you're called.

You also answer
Ilu Afonja, Afonja's town
From the Oyos.

To Fulanis,
You're Garin Alimi,
Alimi's town?
Oh yes!
The Scholars.

A town that is big (and Yoruba speaking)
But detests masquerades.
Horses, own favourites,
Swords (dazzling) are own custom.
Saa Maza gudu, Ilorin Afonja.[5]

The above poem summarizes the origin of present-day Ilorin. Ojo Isekuse, a hunter, was said to have founded Ilorin town, around A.D. 1600.[6] There are two stories regarding where Ojo emanated from. While one version says he came from Oyo-Ile in the former Oyo Empire, the other version insists that Ojo was from Gombe-Ilotta, near Eji.[7] That time, the main implements used by hunters were cullasses, knives, swords, and arrows. So, Ojo was reported to always sharpen his metal tools on certain pieces of rocks around a place now called Ile Bamidele, in Oke-Koto, Ilorin. Wherever he went as a hunter, he would come back to sharpen his implements at Oke-Koto, and gradually, it became his settlement. The name *Ilorin* is shortened from *Ilo irin* (i.e., an object that sharpens metal tools).[8] In other words, Bamidele compound is believed to be the first settlement in what is now Ilorin town.[9] Though the other version is very weak as far as I am concerned, and hardly regarded by the Ilorin people, it will also be interesting to know the story. The narrative says that *Ilorin* actually came from *Ilu erin*, meaning "town of elephants."[10] This version says that the area used to be a forest of elephants before people came to inhabit her. This version uses as evidence a one-time village, which has now merged with the town[11] called *Oko-Erin*.

From the above, and from whatever story we choose to believe, we can now understand that hunters were the first people to inhabit Ilorin. Then gradually more people migrated, most especially, from Oyo-Ile, to settle there. This was because of incessant wars and conflicts in Oyo-Ile around that time.[12] Many people escaped from the wars and made Ilorin their home. People also came from the far North to settle in Ilorin. In fact, it is believed that people from far away area in the present-day Republic of Mali migrated to settle in Ilorin.[13] Even to the local community, they were known as Mali people. They were mainly Muslims, and their religion was described by the local people as *Esin Male*, literally the religion of Mali. This name, which originated from Ilorin people's description of the religion of Islam, was adopted by the whole Yoruba community as the Yoruba name for Islam. The main religions of the Yoruba-speaking people then in Ilorin were Egungun worship, Ogun, Ifa, and other traditional Yoruba worship.

This was the situation around 1796, when Afonja became the Are-Onakankanfo of the Old Oyo Empire army.[14] This post is equivalent to the post of commander-in-chief of the present-day armed forces, which is presently combined with the head of government's post in the present-day Nigeria.[15] In that capacity, Afonja was sent on a war, which, as far as I can believe, was for territorial expansion to a town called *Iwere*. It was during the reign of Alafin Aole.[16] Though Afonja finally captured *Iwere*, he could not claim a clear victory of the war.[17] Consequently, Afonja felt ashamed as many of his armies were killed. What would he say back home? He, therefore, decided to seek after a long-term friend of his, named Ayinla, who he had a report had migrated to Ilorin.[18] A grand warrior that he was, Afonja soon commanded respect and loyalty from the people of his new settlement. People paid him regular homage. I think he was, therefore, pampered by the share respect and generosity of the people who revered him for being the generalissimo of Oyo's army. I believe it was this over generosity of the Ilorin people to Afonja that encouraged him to nurse the ambition of attacking and bringing down the Alafin, or it may be, as many actually believe, the bitterness of being sent on a wrong war, and he thought he had to revenge, so that he, Afonja, could rule over the whole of Oyo Empire. This, of course, is debatable. Would the Are-Onakankanfo then install himself as Alaafin, or would he, if he succeeded, just depose the Alaafin and cause another person from the royal lineage to ascend the throne of his ancestors. This could be an interesting scholarly debate.

As already stated, many migrants from the ancient Mali were already settled in Ilorin, ever before Alfa Alimi or Afonja came there (Afonja and Alimi, of Fulani or Fulbe origin, are the two people, currently occupying legendary status, often acknowledged for the modern-day fame of Ilorin—see the poem on a previous page). It is even argued that it was this group that originally brought Islam to Ilorin.[19] In short, it is a general belief that Islam had been in Ilorin before the Jihad of Uthman Danfodio. Apart from the Malians, some Hausas, Nupes, and Fulanis had already been living in Ilorin before Afonja migrated to the Ilorin and definitely before Alfa Alimi. However, the earlier Ilorin largely spread out on clannish or ethnic group levels. The Mali, Hausa, Fulani, and Nupe were mainly Muslims. There was even a report of a Yoruba Muslim leader called Sholagberu around Okesuna who had settled in Ilorin before Alfa Alimi.[20] The Malians lived in the area presently called *Oke-Male* (meaning "Malians Upland") in Ilorin. The Hausas, Nupes, and Fulanis lived around the present-day Gambari areas.

There are two historical versions that try to explain how Alfa Alimi came to Ilorin. One version says that he had settled in some Yoruba towns around Oyo before moving finally to settle in Ilorin.[21] Another version says, however, that he came straight as an army of the Jihad movement to conquer Ilorin for Islam.[22] The first version, which is the most believed version by the Ilorin people, says that it was Afonja who invited Alimi to bring his solider to help him put the Alafin on his heels. This was promptly done. However, the Muslims' popularity had grown greatly in Ilorin, as the Muslim has helped win a war, and because this singular wonderful performance of the Muslims led by Alimi impressed the settlers who declared for Islam *en masse*.

Trouble erupted between Afonja and Alimi when he tried to convert Afonja to Islam.[23] Alimi supporters, therefore, eliminated Afonja, and Alimi's first son, Abdul Salam, was formally installed as ruler, or Emir, of Ilorin in 1823. All the clans and ethnic groups were, for the first time ever, mobilized together as one town, under one traditional authority of the Emir, which the Ilorin people call

Oba Ilorin. This, thus, marked the establishment of an Emirate tradition in Ilorin, taking after similar Muslim governing system in existence in Sokoto (Sakkwato) and Gwandu Emirate. It was after the emergence of the Ilorin Emirate that Abdul Salam swore allegiance to and obtained a flag of authority from Abdullahi Danfodio, the Emir of Gwandu.[24] Thus, the Islamic system of administration as obtained in Sokoto Caliphate was fully introduced. Another version, however, says that it was Afonja himself who invited Alimi to rule, but Alimi refused, giving as a reason that his mission was purely religious. He said he had no intention nor desire to ascend to a throne. However, Alimi brought his son, Abdul Salam, who later became the first Emir of Ilorin.[25] It is said that Abdul Salam and Alimi were responsible for bringing the hitherto clannish settlements around Ilorin together to form one single community under one general rulership.

Ilorin, therefore, became a multiethnic town with Hausa, Yoruba, Malians,[26] Gobir, Nupe, and Fulani settlers. It is popularly called and adulated as *Ilorin Afonja* and *Garin Alimi* in reference to the two notable individuals whose roles in the development and popularity of the town have been explained above. Ilorin features prominently in Hausa oral songs just as it does in Yoruba *oriki*, and perhaps the most popular Hausa one is the one, I believe, which was included in a Hausa Elementary School Reader, *Karamin Sani*:

'Dan Mali yo, Mali yo!	Oh, Mali Children!
Mali yo!	Oh, Mali!
'Dan Mali o nawa!	My Mali children!
Mali yo!	Oh, Mali!
Ya je ina ne!	Where does he (do they) go!
Mali yo!	Oh, Mali!
Ya je Ilori	He's gone to Ilori
Mali yo!	Oh, Mali!
Ba sai dawo ba	He won't be back
Mali yo!	Oh, Mali!
Sai a watan gobe	Un till next month
Mali yo!	Oh, Mali!
Gobe da labari	Tomorrow, lots of stories to tell
Mali yo!	Oh, Mali!
Jibi da labarai!	The day after, so many stories to tell!
Mali yo!	Oh, Mali!
Karkad'a mu gani	Dance a bit, and let's see (if you can)
Alis Alis Alis	(moving the waist) Alis, Alis, Alis!

Ilorin is, to the Hausa, *Ilori*, and this community name appears in both Yoruba and Hausa folklore. For the young Hausa girls in the above folk performance, they dance to the song and twist their hips during an evening moonlight play. This song is so popular among school-going Hausa pupils that it attains a popular art status, especially among young girls playing the children games and hide-and-seek dramatic performance on the open field. Their folk hero has gone to *Ilori* and would not return for another month! *Ilori* and Mali feature prominently in the song, and the *Ilori* ancestry, to the Hausa folklore, is linked much more to Mali than to any other ethnic lineage, as no mention is made of Ilorin's relationship to the Oyo Yoruba in the song. The fact that the Yoruba people call Islam *Esin Male*, which is another way of saying, *Esin Mali*, the religion of Mali people, shows that the Yoruba acknowledges the Mali's heritage in Ilorin. It is also an evidence of Ilorin's role in the spread of Islam among the Yoruba areas of Nigeria. The fact that the Yoruba would choose a name derived from Ilorin's history and culture as a name of a religion as important and impactful among the Yoruba people as Islam shows the importance of place that Ilorin occupies in the sensitivity of the Yoruba people. A whole part of Ilorin, more than half of the size of the geographical Ilorin, is called *Oke-Male,* Mali Area, and a traditional title of Ilorin till date, for one of its two most senior Imams, is, by heritage and ancestry, the one called *Imam Male*, the Imam of Mali ancestry/origin.

Ilorin has been known as a city of brave and courageous warriors in history and people known for conquering many towns and kingships in wars. A play by Isiaka Aliagan, *Oba Mama*, presents one of such episodes when an Ilorin Emir, Oba Mama, and his chiefs could not agree because the chiefs preferred wars to the new Oba's diplomacy. Ilorin was involved in many interethnic wars during most of the Emirs, especially Emir Aliyu (fourth Emir). These wars included one sour war, the Jalimi war that Ilorin lost to Ikirun. It was a known fact that Ikirun was aided by the Ibadan.[27] The Ilorin people believed that Ikirun was no match at all with Ilorin and needed to seek for another city's support in order to prevail. In a nutshell, the Ilorins were known to be great warriors. That is why it is said that "Sword is Ilorin's custom," *oko loro ibe.*

For the smooth administration of Ilorin land, it was divided into several units with Baloguns and Magaji Aare as heads of different wards and units. There were also other lesser Magajis, Alangua and Baales spread around villages and the suburbs. The Baloguns were four, and from their names (Baba ólógún), they were head warriors:

Alanamu, Ajikobi, Gambari, and Fulani. They are army chiefs of the land.[28] The Baloguns are so powerful that occasionally there are reports of tension between them and the Emir. Many traditional titles are (Waziri, Turaki, Dan Madami, Zanna, Tafida, etc) given by the Emir to deserving indigenes of Ilorin into the twenty-first century. Alimi's other male children, and later, children of the substitute Emirs of Ilorin, were appointed as Daudu, Baale and Magaji to different districts and villages under Ilorin Emirate.[29] All these places under Ilorin land, therefore, fall within the scope of this discussion. Most use of the name Ilorin in this project, therefore, refers to the whole of Ilorin Emirate unless otherwise stated.

Social and economic activities of Ilorin people

Ilorin town has an identity as a Muslim town. There is no other dominant culture in Ilorin, at least as far as its people are concerned, other than the Islamic culture. Yet, Yoruba oral traditions and songs and cultural activities of the ethnic groups that brought Islam to Ilorin (i.e. Hausa, Fulani, Gobir, and Nupe) abound in the community. Most of these are largely traditional African performances, but many are now being used to promote Islam and Ilorin Muslim identity. More and more as time progresses, cultural elements that Ilorin Muslim scholars see as contradicting the hegemony of Islam were preached against and most probably eliminated. Many practices would definitely be easily found underground and unable to face the flourishing public faces of Islam in the community. This is often the case in many areas of Ilorin Emirate; however, areas like Sao have strong presence of Yoruba traditional religion and later Christianity. As for Ilorin town, the only prevailing community festivals and ceremonies into the twenty-first century are the Eid'l Fitir (Odun Awe), Eid'l Adha (Odun Ileya), Nikka (Iwayo 'wedding'), (Suna) naming ceremonies, and so on. There are many oral artists who entertain people during such ceremonies, and these oral artists performing genres originated from traditional African socioreligious roots are now performed in the modern Muslim city, still making references to elements of Yoruba religion and spirituality, but oftentimes in such ways that they do not offend the sensibility of the dominant Muslim culture. Some of the oral performances also came with Muslim traditions and are amalgamation of Yoruba or Hausa traditional performances and Islamic expressive traditions. These Ilorin genres include the *Baalu*, the *Were*, the *Waka*, the Molo, the *Sekere*, and the *Agbè*. It also includes the Dàdàkúàdá, which this work will discuss in a greater detail.

Ilorin is an important commercial center that maximizes the advantage of its geographical position as the gateway between north and south, at least before and during colonization. In the twenty-first century, Ilorin Motor Parks are always full of people moving to and from different parts of the country. Traders from other communities bring their goods from the South and traders come from the North to buy them, so Ilorin as always served as a kind of meeting point. Before the new Ilorin Juma'at mosque was built at its present position,[30] a very big traditional market that used to operate both morning and night was situated there. I remember myself always liked to attend that market, and I enjoyed, as a child, just roaming it and enjoying and learning from young and old. Indeed, that market was always busy! Olaoye reported an American observer who was impressed by the enormous extent of Ilorin and the cosmopolitan roar of its market as far back as 1857 to have described Ilorin as "One of the greatest enterpots of Central Africa."[31] The Ilorin people are mostly farmers. The savannah grassland vegetation of Ilorin is highly favorable to this. Ilorin farmers produce yams, cassava, guinea corn, groundnut, maize, and cotton.[32]

Traditional weaving is another important occupation of the Ilorin indigenes. Both men and women, young and old, weave cloths popularly called *Aso-Ofi*. This is introduced to Ilorin from Iseyin.[33] Other occupations like pottery, leather works, blacksmithing, and dyeing also abound as traditional occupation of Ilorin.[34] Professional driving is among modern occupation that is popular in Ilorin. Because of the geography location of the city, private businesses provide small and big cars and lorries that connect many cities, especially Nigeria state capitals, and also Lagos and Abuja. It is, therefore, common to Ilorin people whose families have produced generations of professional drivers.

As the capital city of one of the Nigerian states (Kwara State), Ilorin has the advantage of housing government offices and playing host to state workers and thus attracting businesses and public services such as restaurants, telecommunication, print and electronic media, and educational institutions including elementary schools, high schools, junior colleges, a polytechnique, and a research university. Ilorin, therefore, plays host to workers from across the Nigeria who have built houses in the outskirt of the city and have taken Ilorin as their homes. The Ilorin middle class, mainly those who have acquired Western education, also work in offices and as teachers and technicians. In short, in both the areas of occupation and housing, Ilorin can be divided into two: traditional occupations and modern occupations, and traditional city areas and city outskirt or new city extension areas. Ilorin city continues to expand from all sides, especially the North, South, West, and East. However, most of the West expansion is due to nonindigenous Ilorin people buying lands and constructing new houses and businesses. The expansion in the North is largely by Ilorin indigenes but also includes contemporary migrants into the city. From the South and the East, there seems to be equal percentages of businesses and residential expansions, and of natives and immigrants. It is interesting, therefore, that while traditional areas of Ilorin have largely retained their traditional cultural outlooks, the extension areas present opportunities for migrants and natives to develop businesses and new residential areas.

There are only a few industries in Ilorin town, mainly sugar production, soap industry, food industry, iron roofs, nail industry (Camwire), pharmaceutical companies, and they employ a fair population of natives and immigrants. Majority of middle-class people, therefore, work in government offices where many also serve as messengers and office cleaners. The hotel industry is perhaps among the most popular ones in Ilorin, involving private and public participation. The Kwara State government owns the most popular hotel in Ilorin, the Kwara Hotel. Yet, other famous hotels include Yebumot, Phoenix, Nektal, Millinium, Whitefield, Fresh, Circular Hotel, and many more.

The most perennial problem in Ilorin is drinking water. The majority of the city depends on the Asa Dam for their water, which is largely inadequate. It is often common, therefore, to see people with buckets and Jeri cans looking for water in the traditional areas. Wells, boreholes, taps, and bottle water are among popular means of drinking water in Ilorin.

Finally, Ilorin presents very interesting cultural and social opportunities for both indigenes and nonindigenes. From the Islamic cultural activities, to the multilingual opportunities, to the traditions and cultures brought by the new immigrants from all parts of Nigeria, including substantial population of Igbo, non-Ilorin Yoruba and Hausa, and other language groups from across Nigeria, to the influences of Arabic Idadi, Iptidahi and Sanawi Schools such as Al-Mahd and Dar-Alhulum and all levels of western education schools, a major university, the University of Ilorin and its Teaching Hospital, Al-Hikma University, Crown-Hill University, living in Ilorin in the twenty-first century can bring a great thrill of life to family and the individual. Apart from the ethnic artistic forms and performances that abound in all its corners, Islam has brought a different kind of color and fame to the city. The Ilorin Central Mosque is a center of attraction to visitors from all over the world. The palace of the Muslim Emir is imposing and also has very strong spiritual and temporal significances for the people. Muslim festivals and oral performances have also put Ilorin on the map of one of the most culturally vibrant cities in Nigeria. As a capital city of Kwara State and host of a Federal Secretariat, Federal High Court and Court of Appeal, and many electronic-age facilities, Ilorin combines major Afro-Islamic traditions with significant Western presence. Through its songs and musical instrumentation, both Islam and Western presence have influenced Dàdàkúàdá genre, the main subject of this work. Contemporary technology has impacted Dàdàkúàdá in many ways. Yet, I am not suggesting that the native and the ordinary see every twenty-first-century intervention in Ilorin as a great excitement. Indeed, what I call "globalization influences" have created tensions for ordinary people in the ways they struggle to retain their local culture and identity, but this book is not the forum for such a discussion (see my book, *Globalization, Oral Performance, and African Traditional Poetry*, 2018).

Notes

1 R.A. Olaoye, "The Ilorin Emirate and British Ascebdency 1897–1918: An Overview of the Early Phase of Ilorin Provincial Administration," M.A. Thesis, U of Ilorin (1984).
2 Ibid.
3 This was divided into three when 12 local government areas were created in Kwara State in 1967. Ilorin Emirate used to be a much larger political area during the first republic when Nigeria had three regions and Ilorin was in the northern region. Most of the areas like Kabba, Igbonna, and more marked under Ilorin Emirate were distinct ethnic groups and not Ilorin.
4 The map was adapted from the Ph.D. Thesis of H.S.A. Dan Mole—"The Frontier Emirate: A History of Islam in Ilorin," U of Birmingham (1980): 188.
5 This was my poem published in *The Herald* (9 May 1987): 14 and republished in *Sunday Concord* (16 August 1987): 8.
6 E.O. Amao, "Baluu Chants and Songs in Ilorin," Kwara State, M.A. Thesis, U of Ibadan (1983): 2.
7 Ibid., 2–3.
8 H.B. Karmen-Hodge, *Gazetteer of Ilorin Province* (London: George Allein & Unwin Ltd., 1929): 63.
9 Ibid.
10 Ibid.
11 Ibid.
12 It is reported that Oyo engaged in many wars between A.D. 1790 and 1850.
13 A. Na'Allah, "Arabic and Islamic Education in Ilorin," in *Unilorin Pedagoque* (1985): 37.
14 R.A. Olaoye, "The Ilorin Emirate and British Ascedency 1897–1918: An overview of the Early Phase of Ilorin Provincial Administration," M.A. Thesis, U of Ilorin (1984): 5–7.
15 Right from the time Nigeria became a republic to the present moment, the head of the Nigerian government is also addressed as commander-in-chief of the Nigerian armed forces. This is clearly in the 1979 and 1999 Nigerian constitutions.

16 R.A. Olaoye, "The Ilorin Emirate and the British Ascendency 1897–1918: An Overview of the Early Phase of Ilorin Provincial Administration," M.A. Thesis, U of Ilorin (1984): 5–7.
17 Ibid.
18 Ibid.
19 A. Na'Allah. "Arabic and Islamic Education in Ilorin," in *Unilorin Pedagoque* (1985): 37–50. See also Adam Abdullahi Al-Ilori's *History of Nigeria*, originally written in Arabic. Strongly recommended for understanding Ilorin history from Ilorin indigene's and oral traditions perspectives.
20 R.A. Olaoye, "The Ilorin Emirate and the British Ascendency 1897–1918: An Overview of the Early Phase of Ilorin Provincial Administration," M.A. Thesis, U of Ilorin (1984): 6–7.
21 Ibid.
22 Personal interview with Sa'adu Iman, 22 September 1987.
23 R.A. Olaoye, "The Ilorin Emirate and the British Ascendency 1897–1918: An Overview of the Early Phase of Ilorin Provincial Administration," M.A. Thesis, U of Ilorin (1984): 7.
24 Ibid., 10–11.
25 Ibid.
26 The exact ethnic name of the Malians is not known.
27 E.O. Amao, "Baluu Chants and Songs in Ilorin," Kwara State, M.A. Thesis, U of Ibadan (1983).
28 R.A. Olaoye, "The Ilorin Emirate and the British Ascendency 1897–1918: An Overview of the Early Phase of Ilorin Provincial Administration," M.A. Thesis, U of Ilorin (1984): 17–18.
29 This practice still goes on even in the twenty-first century. Though the Ilorin Emirate was divided into many local government areas at different times, the Emirate at this time contains Ilorin West, Ilorin East, Ilorin South, Moro, and Asa local government areas (the Emir of Ilorin still appoints *Baales* and *Magajis* for all the surrounding Ilorin villages).
30 The mosque was formally opened by the then civilian president of Nigeria, Alhaji Shehu Shangari, on 20 June 1980.
31 R.A. Olaoye, "The Ilorin Emirate and the British Ascendency 1897–1918: An overview of the Early Phase of Ilorin Provincial Administration," M.A. Thesis, U of Ilorin (1984): 4.
32 E.O. Amao, "Baluu Chants and Songs in Ilorin," Kwara State, M.A. Thesis, U of Ibadan (1983): 8.
33 Ibid.
34 Ibid., 8.

2 Performance, poetry, and oral traditions overview

In *Globalization, Oral Performance, and African Traditional Poetry,* I have done most of what I would have wanted to do in this chapter, and I therefore like to refer readers, again, to that book for a review of oral literature scholarship generally. I will try not to repeat myself here. However, the Homeric poems perhaps present one of the oldest opportunities in the West for scholars of oral performance to research performance history and characteristics of oral traditions. Without question, Ruth Finnegan, Isidore Okpewho, and many other pioneer scholars of African oral traditions have been very important to the type of scholarly rigor contemporary African scholars who have devoted to oral performance scholarship in Africa. The strength of Babalola's work on Ijala and the depth of Okpewho's work on Myth and Epic are some important examples. African orality scholarship has remained ever strong. Hitherto at the height of colonial education in Africa, it was "uncivilized" to think of African oral tradition as worthy of any scholarly attention. Thanks to the decolonization project of Ngugi and his colleagues at the University of Nairobi, and thanks to the pioneer work that Parry and Lord had done on the Homeric poems, and the extremely timely intervention by scholars of African indigenous languages, religions, cultures, and traditions such as Bascom, Finnegan, Bolaji Idowu, and their contemporaries, and the dedication of Isidore Okpewho and his contemporaries, even thanks to the book, *Orality and Literacy* by Walter Ong, despite its shortcomings, African scholarly tradition in critical imagination and literature have been liberated as true scholarship; with pride, many now refer to African traditional sources as roots of multidisciplinary knowledge, critical thoughts, and protean ideas, as done by Abiola Irele in his *African Imagination.*

Ilorin, the area covered by this project, is not just a Yoruba town; it is a multiethnic town. The history of Ilorin is discussed in Chapter 1. In short, Ilorin combines the richness of all the ethnic groups concerned to become even richer culturally. Of course, the advent of Islam brought great changes in the lives of the Ilorin people of the time, and more so the Ilorin people of the twenty-first century, most especially because over 98% of the indigenous of Ilorin town now profess Islam. Yet, the pre-Islamic culture of Ilorin has not been completely eradicated. A lot has been eliminated, and many new forms have replaced them so that when we count the number from both ends, we shall see that nothing is lost in number, after all. My *Globalization* book (2018: 36–41) presents a summary of what is termed "General Outlook of Oral Literature" and "Ilorin Oral Literature," respectively, and I do not seek to repeat those here. However, I will need to expand on that discussion so that an in-depth understanding of oral literature and specifically the oral genres of Ilorin may be possible.

I think it is appropriate in the twenty-first century to treat with caution Parry's[1] conclusion on the composition of oral verse that

> a series of patterns of the formula, therefore, is by itself far beyond the power of any one man. The epithets, the metaphorical expressions, the phrases for the binding clauses, the formulas for running the sentences over from one verse to another … is beyond whatever supreme genius.[2]

It is not that the importance of formulaic for the oral singer is diminished by the advent of some kind of "super-technology" or by the inherent ability of the poet to create new and original patterns and styles. Yet, whether then or now, I would believe that every talented poet would use his or her own original metaphorical expressions, phrases, and even help in creating new words and terminologies, despite the fact that they may have maintained performance patterns of their ancestors. A dedication to ancestral patterns among traditional African oral singer, for whatever reason this may be, does not take away their talent at, and actual creation of, newer patterns during any performance. It is also not beyond any oral poet to, therefore, think new and to want a different performance style to carry their new, or even at that, old songs. It seems to me, therefore, that Parry may be taking the idea of "no one supreme genius" too far! Why would Parry even think creating a new performance pattern was more difficult than thinking out a new theme, or why may we think it is easier for a poet to use an existing pattern than creating new ones? Why is a poet performing new songs not find it easy, and I actually think he or she does find it easy, to use new patterns to present those songs? Would it be correct to always insist that oral performers are helpless when it comes to breaking away from a performance tradition passed over to them from a previous generation? More so, what is ancestral tradition or style today started from one ancestor one day, and that day when it started, it was new and original. Even when Ilorin oral poets use ancestral patterns and styles in their songs in the twenty-first century, it does not limit their ability to initiate new styles of their own which would also pass over to other generations in future. For example, Ilorin Quranic recitation patterns, from an important verbal art of Ilorin, were recently boosted with the Imam Bashir pattern that was newly developed and added to them with the selection of a new Imam Fulani of Ilorin. The Imam Bashir pattern of Quranic recitation will eventually become an ancestral pattern as it passes to new and future generation!

However, from the many scholarly responses to what we can comfortably call Parry and Lord's Formulaic Theory (Foley[3] is an example of leading American scholars who have contributed to the Formulaic discussions) and from the many efforts to relate to oral performances from across the world, one can conclude that Parry's and Lord's efforts are a marking point in the study of oral poetry and especially its cross-cultural scholarly discussions in the world. Yes, this is not an influence only in the West, but it also spreads its impact on the studies of oral traditions in Africa, especially in Africa's Western tertiary institutions.

What, in simple words, are the rudiments of Parry's and Lord's studies? Albert Lord, influenced by the efforts of Parry (who was his teacher—thus the belief that many of Lord's contributions were also Parry's), tries to show the similarity between the thematic inconsistencies in Homer (deconstructing Homer?) and the southern slave epic singer's songs.[4] While briefly discussing their works, I referred to Parry and these other scholars as "important European scholars of oral forms" (see *Globalization*, Palgrave, 2018, 37). Parry observes that the inconsistencies that are seen "stem from the thematic and formulaic structure of the oral epic poetry."[5] Lord says that theme determines the style of an oral poetry and insists that the theme of a poem is as important as the performance pattern in which the poem is rendered. He believes therefore that "Compositions of the oral singers in Yugoslavia relied largely on the stock of formulas and themes that had become fixed in the creator's head."[6] Definitely both Parry and Lord are old literature, but even twenty-first-century scholarship might commit the same mistake of believing that a poetic theme would always influence performance structure of the poem. The idea that all that oral poets do is to follow one pattern passed to them from their ancestors whenever they adopt a particular theme or sing certain particular theme, whether or not they adopt a given pattern, is devaluing the superior creative genius of the traditional oral poet of any culture. It was this yardstick that led both Parry and Lord to believe that the pattern and style of oral poetry are no creation of any one person, but what has been passed from one generation to another and has been "fixed" in the poet's mind. While I agree that patterns are passable (and actually many times passed) from one generation to another, I totally reject the idea that any one oral poet may not, at will, create a new and different pattern or style of his or her own. Lord adds that oral poems do reflect extensive narrative patterning and further argues that any formula found in a written poem "must be an emulation by the literary writer for it is easy to copy by those writers who have listened to it frequently."[7] While I am not arguing whether writers emulate oral poets or not (they certainly do so in modern Africa!), I would vigorously disagree with the discourse that may inadvertently present traditional poets as helpless, weak, and often dependent on ready-made words and patterns to perform. Some of the Ilorin poets discussed in this book are clear evidence of divergence patterns and styles even when many of them perform during the same historical period. While some performance and compositional patterns are transferred from ancestral forms, many are new and unique. I have seen on performance fields that African oral poets would refuse to fit into the models of Western trained musicians who on pubic performance would perform in an imitation (a bit similar to dubbing in films) to the replay of their records tracing their recorded voices and pretending at times that they are on spontaneous performance outings. Such is the use of electronic technology that traditional African oral singers may find as an abuse of modern digital advancement and technical enhancement of oral culture.

In terms of Ilorin traditional oral forms, the few pre-Islamic oral poetry genres that survive to this day have been greatly metamorphosed into new forms, mainly doing away with things considered un-Islamic. Not many people have conducted studies into Ilorin traditional oral arts, and therefore, very little literature exists on the pre-Islamic poetry of Ilorin. In fact, my effort to locate literature on Ilorin oral art yielded few results.[8] Most of the works done are undergraduate long essays or graduate master's or doctoral theses. Ajayi, Yenkini Ajibaye conducted a research on *Asa* for his M.A. (Yoruba) thesis in 1982 in the University of Ibadan.[9] Describing his work, he says,

> This is the first systematic study of Asa artists, a group of ininer-ant Jesters in Yoruba society, especially in Ilorin area of Kwara State.[10]

Also, Amao, Elkanah Oladoja writes on "Baluu Chants and Songs in Ilorin, Kwara State" for his M.A. thesis in 1983 (also in University of Ibadan). Apart from the above two, I also laid my hands on two newspaper articles on Ilorin traditional poetry.[11]

Asa is one of the oral arts of Ilorin. It is a verbal art. It is rendered in poetry but mostly like a normal speech form.[12] Ajayi lists the characteristic features of *Asa* artists. He says that an *Asa* does not feel offended when shunned or molested. In the olden days, he says, *Asa* artists had common dress by which they were recognized. The word *Asa* itself is used to describe a man or a woman without shame.[13]

Another pre-Islamic art is the *Agbe* art. The artists are called *Alagbe*. They are known for their acrobatic displays. This music used to be the most popular in Ilorin.[14] The main musical instrument is *Agbe* (the gourd). This music is still very much in Ilorin, but it is not as popular as it was reported to be in the olden days. The fans are greatly decreasing.[15]

Another pre-Islamic art is *Ere Baalu*. Both Yekini Ajibaye and Amao Elkanah refer to this art as a modern development.[16] In his seminar work during the 1983, Amao, most especially, says that it was developed about 50 years ago.[17] He does not justify his claim with any reason other than the name of the art. My findings, however, reveal otherwise. *Ere Baalu* has been in Ilorin ever before the advent of Islam.[18] It is true that it was not called *Baalu* then, but the kinds of songs, dance, and artists were very much around. Also, unlike what Amao says, the people never have a balloon in mind when they tag this play *Baalu*.[19] Among the Ilorin Yorubas, Baalu means airplane.[20] It is possible that they had a balloon in mind when they called it airplane in the first instance, but that is not synonymous to having the same thing in mind when they call this play. So, the name *Baalu* is derived from the adopted name for airplane.[21] The dance to *Ere Baalu* is truly as if a plane is flying. In *Ere Baalu*, the lead singer and all members of her chorus groups are women. The drummers are men. There is also a *Boto*. He passes comments and throws jokes in on different topics of the songs. A *Boto*, here, can either be a man or a woman.

Sekere is another very interesting pre-Islamic oral art of Ilorin. The only musical instruments are smaller gourds that have well-rounded beads around them. The gourds are shaken and thrown round and round to give rhythmic sound to the songs.[22]

Ilorin also has rara chant which, according to Omoekee Amao, a notable Ilorin artist, is different from rara Oyo.[23] Amao says he chants rara anytime he likes during his performance. Rara is a one man, one drum poetry. Most rara poets do not beat drum to their rara. There are few rara artists in Ilorin today.

Dàdàkúàdá is another very interesting pre-Islamic poetry of Ilorin. It is the primary topic of this book and much shall be discussed on it in later chapters.

Most of the post-Islamic oral arts are greatly religious and are used in religious ceremonies. Apart from *Kakaki, Waka, Were, Egbe Iyawo,* and *Ere Olomooba*, no one has identified other post-Islamic oral arts in his writings so far,[24] until my article was published in a national daily.[25] Which identified as most popular and most respected oral art in Ilorin, to include *Bandiri, Orin Esin, Orin Makondoro*, the chanting of the holy Quran, and Yoruba chanting of Islamic preachers in Ilorin.[26]

Waka is a darling poetry of Ilorin people (read *Cultural Plurality and Globalization* for a more comprehensive discussion of *Waka*). People are reminded of their religious duties through it. There are three types of Ilorin Waka art. The first type, which is the only one I will present here, is employed to entertain people on the eve of Volimat day. The lead artists of this type of *Waka* are usually very knowledgeable in Quran, Hadith, and Islamic history. This type of Waka is usually in groups. Each group is made up of a leader and a chorus subgroup comprising of as many as 20 or more members. Ajisodun and Dodo are ex-exponents of this Waka. Dodo Agbarere, Alhaji Labeka of Idiape, Alhaja Wahabi of Okelele, Alhaja Afusat Onisese of Omoda, and Alhaja Mero Ladi of Sakamo are among legendary Waka artists who have lived.[27]

Kakaki royal art is another oral art in Ilorin. The instrument used here is the long metal trumpet called Kakaki (from which the art got its name). The Kakaki royal band is exclusively for the Emir of Ilorin. It is, however, now popular in the courts of many Yoruba Obas. These include the Alafin of Oyo, Olubadan of Ibadan, Alake of Egblaland, the Ogega of Ikere-Ekiti, and Olowo of Owo.[28] It is even said that this art is introduced into Yorubaland through Ilorin around 1823 A.D. during the establishment of the Ilorin Emirate.[29] That is to say, it is brought from the Hausa and Fulani lands of the farther north of Nigeria.

Another post-Islamic art of Ilorin is the *Were*. It started as a religious poetry and still remains so wherever it is performed. The *Were* chants are used to wake people up for early morning food (Saari) during the Ramadan—Muslim holy month of fasting. *Agogo*, bell, small *sakara* drum, and any object that was sure to give a high sound when beaten were introduced to *Were*.[30] This was meant to generate enough sound to wake people from bed to eat in readiness for the next day fasting. It is *Were* that now develops to *Fuji*.

Toobeeni is a dance and music. The artists here use *Bembe* drum. In fact, the most popular name for this art is *Bembe*. Very few people recognize it as *Toobeeni*. Flutists and smaller Kakaki artists also follow the Bembe drummers to entertain the housewives, usually when the Toobeeni artists perform during weddings and naming ceremonies.

Bandiri is a completely religious oral art. The Quadiriyya group of Muslims chant it. The songs are both Islamic and Arabic. In Alfa-Nda area of Ilorin, an annual ceremony is held for the remembrance of Sheikh-Abdul-Qadir, the leader of the group. The type of drum used is called *Bandiri* and from it the art derives its name. The Bandiri drum is exactly like the present-day sakara drum in form. However, it is three to four times bigger than a sakara drum.

Orin Makondoro is another very interesting oral art. The pupils and Mallams of the Agbaji Makondoro School and its disciples chant it. They chant their songs during weddings, namings, or other ceremonies of their members. Drumming of any kind is forbidden to this poetry.

We also have the chants of grand Islamic preachers in Yoruba language. Such poetry is adopted to enable preachers reach the grassroots. The Malians recognize the potentiality of poetry in reaching grassroots.[31] Such grand Mallams like Kokewu Kobere and Ajongolo[32] are known for this. Again, there is no drumming whatsoever to such chants.

Chants and recitations of the Holy Quran are also popular art of Ilorin. In fact, they can be described as the most popular and most common of all Ilorin oral arts. The recitation is done with beautiful and melodious voices. Four voices or styles of recitation are traditional to Ilorin. These are Imam Fulani Solihu voice, the Adabiyya/Kamaliyya voice, the Adam/Yahaya voice, and the traditional "heee voice."[33] I have devoted a bit more time to the discussion of the local Quranic recitation voices in Ilorin in another work (*Africanity, Islamicity and Performativity: Identity in the House of Ilorin*).

Finally, two other performing arts are not only traditional to but are also very popular in Ilorin: *Egbe Iyawo* and *Ere Olomooba*. The *Egbe Iyawo* is performed during wedding ceremonies only as part of the wedding rituals in Ilorin. The dramatists here (not professionals but everyday person in Ilorin) include those in the age group of the bride, the age group of the bridegroom, and the two celebrants themselves. *Egbe Iyawo* is usually performed on Fridays and Saturdays, when the weeklong wedding activities are coming to an end.[34] The word *Egbe Iyawo* means "the bride's group." The major musical instrument used by the performers is the *Kengbe* gourd. This is put between the laps and beaten rhythmically to the songs and the dance. Egbe Iyawo involves a number of hide-and-seek games with the bride's group hiding the *Iyawo* (bride) while the *Egbe Oko-Iyawo* (the bridegroom's group) pursuing and searching everywhere to seek them out. The seek-out and subsequent release[35] of *Iyawo* marks the end of the play, in jubilation.

The *Ere Olomooba* is a "Princess dance." It is mainly a dancing display. Aged and elderly women who are relations of the Emir perform *Ere Olomooba*.[36] This is done when the Emir's son or daughter or any of his relation is doing wedding ceremony. It is also performed, at times, during naming ceremonies. *Odo* (Mortal) is out in the middle, and water is poured to its mid-level. A Calabash is then out with its back to the sky. This is beaten to supply sounds to the rhythm of the songs. Except those beating the Calabash, all others form a circle and dance majestically to the rhythm. They throw their hands in slow motion while dancing. Anyone of them can lead their songs. Habibah Lukman Adam in her research into *Ere Olomooba* traces it to many palaces in Yorubaland, including Erin Ile. Her work is a very good documentation of the history, performance techniques, and aesthetic features of *Ere Olomooba* in traditional Yoruba community. It also covers important influences on the performance and the differences of its features from one palace to the other. While the Ilorin one has Fulani-Yoruba connotation and heritage because of the Fulani origin of the Ilorin Kingship, the Erin Ile *Ere Olomooba* is rooted solely in Yoruba heritage with strong features of Yoruba cultural and metaphysical contents (see Habibah Lukman Adam, "Ere Olomooba").

Notes

1 P. Milman, "Studies in the Epic Technique of Oral Verse-Making: Homer and Homeric Style," in *Harvard Studies in Classical Philosophy*, 41 (1930): 73.
2 A. Dandatti, "The Role of an Oral Singer in Hausa-Fulani Society: A Case Study of Mamman Shatta," Dissertation, Indiana U (1978).
3 See, for example, his discussion in, John Miles Foley, *How to Read an Oral Poem* (Urbana: U of Illinois P, 2002).
4 A.B. Lord, *The Singer of Tales* (Harvard: Harvard UP, 1960): 5–50.
5 P. Milman, "Studies in the Epic Technique of Oral Verse-Making: Homer and Homeric Style," in *Harvard Studies in Classical Philosophy*, 41 (1930): 73.
6 A.B. Lord, *The Singer of Tales* (Harvard: Harvard UP, 1960): 5–50.
7 A.B. Lord, "Perspective on Recent Work on Oral Literature," *Forum for Modern Language Studies*, 10 (July 1974): 187–210.

8 I made a thorough search of necessary publications in Unilorin and Ibadan University Libraries.

9 That research is titled "Asa: A Public Entertainment in Ilorin Area of Kwara State" and made in 1982.

10 Y.A. Ajayi, "Asa: A Public Entertainment in Ilorin Area of Kwara State," M.A. Thesis, U of Ibadan (1982): in the abstract.

11 The articles are written by me (i.e. "Dàdàkúàdá: The music of Ilorin," in *Nigerian Herald* [5 November 1985]: 6 and "Oral and Performatic Arts of Ilorin," [Serials I &II] in *The Herald* [8 September 1987]: 9, and [12 September 1987]: 13.

12 Y.A. Ajayi, "Asa: A Public Entertainment in Ilorin Area of Kwara State," M.A. Thesis, U of Ibadan (1982): 221–22.

13 Personal interview with Saaratu Odee, 2 September 1987.

14 Ibid.

15 One hardly sees Agbè artists in Ilorin those days. They are limited to around Oloje and Ilorin villages (Oko Ilorin).

16 E.O. Amao, "Baluu Chants and Songs in Ilorin, Kwara State," M.A. Thesis, U of Ibadan (1983): 17.

17 Ibid.

18 All Baalu artists and the fans I interviewed agreed on that.

19 E.O. Amao, "Baalu Chants and Songs in Ilorin, Kwara State," M.A. Thesis, U of Ibadan (1983): 13.

20 I am an Ilorin Yoruba.

21 This is attested to by the Baalu artists and some fans I interviewed.

22 Personal interview with Saaratu Odee, 2 September 1987.

23 Personal interview with Omoekee Amao, 8 August 1987.

24 Both A.Y. Ajayi and E.O. Amao identify only those poetry as the indigenous oral arts of Ilorin.

25 A. Na'Allah, "Oral and Performatic Arts of Ilorin," in *The Herald* (8 September 1987): 9.

26 Ibid.

27 E.O. Amao, "Baluu Chants and Songs in Ilorin, Kwara State," M.A. Thesis, U of Ibadan (1983): 6.

28 M.A. Omibiyi-Obidike, "Islam Influence on Yoruba Music," in *Africa Notes*, VIII.2 (1981): 47.

29 Ibid.

30 Sikiru Ayinde Barister (now deceased) and Alhaji Kolawole Rasaki are popularly believed to have developed *Fuji* from *Were*. They were both based in Lagos. See Debra Klien (2007), online source: https://www.researchgate.net/publication/313970596_Fuji_Indigenous_and_Islamic_Popular_Music_Fusions_in_Nigeria. Klien seems to credit Barister alone with the finding of Fuji.

31 This same method was adopted by Sheikh Uthman Danfodio and other Sokoto Jihadits in winning people to their cause. See A. Na'Allah, "Arts and Revolution in Africa," in *The Punch* (15 January 1986): 9.

32 Personal interview with Alhaji Salisu Kokewu Kobere, 12 September 1987.

33 A. Na'Allah, "Oral and Performatic Arts of Ilorin" in *The Herald* (8 September 1987): 9.

34 Traditionally, Friday is the wedding day for the bridegroom, Thursday being that of the bride, who is then conveyed to her husband house that Thursday night or Friday early morning, with the entire marriage ceremony coming to an end on Saturday evening with Igba Iyawo. The whole event has now changed in Ilorin; most now fix marriage ceremony to weekend, often only one day!

35 I have watched and participated in the performance several times.

36 Personal interview with Saaratu Odee, 2 September 1987.

3 Developmental stages of Dàdàkúàdá

In tracing the development history of Dàdàkúàdá, I have relied very heavily on oral history and conducted interviews of ordinary people as well as leading oral artists in Ilorin. Luckily, some of the artists have enjoyed longevity, and some of those I interviewed who are currently in their seventies started apprenticeship and professional performance when they were only children. Yet, others among those I interviewed, like Omoekee Amao, Odolaye Aremu, and Aremu Ose, have now become deceased. With the passing of Aremu Ose in 2007 shortly after his songs where he criticized a set of Ilorin political leadership and set out expectations for Obasanjo's second term as President of Nigeria, it dawned on me the urgency of getting this study out and of continuing my research in this area while a few of the elderly poets who carry the memory of its unique history are still alive. With just a bit reflection, I was struck by the alarming rate at which globalization was now forcing traditional forms to conform to Western models. My book on globalization (2018) could therefore not wait and took substantial materials from what I had originally intended for this book.[1]

The mystery about the origin of Dàdàkúàdá and the interest easily generated in knowing the truth about its development are due to the strong Muslim status of Ilorin community in Nigeria. Ilorin has always been in the news as a center of Islamic learning, and sometimes even controversial reports have emerged about its Yoruba history and its Islamic-cum-Hausa-Fulani influences. It is little wonder then that a performance genre like Dàdàkúàdá, which is highly suspected to be rooted in traditional Yoruba spiritual and metaphysical essences, would generate people's interest whenever materials are presented about its origin. How can a community be so identified with strong Islamic devotion and yet be seen as projecting a strong performance culture thought to have taken roots from traditional African cultic heritage! I would not be exaggerating when I say that in the whole of Yoruba community of the twenty-first century hardly can one find other oral performance genre that has retained its linguistic flavor and ethnic manifestations like the Dàdàkúàdá genre! Yet, as we shall discuss later in this work, the Dàdàkúàdá poets have also negotiated so well a place for themselves and for their poetry in which the Ilorin Islamic sensibility is acknowledged and accommodated in their poetry. Even where there continues to be suspicion and mistrust between traditional Dàdàkúàdá poets and the Ilorin Islamic scholars, no danger is visible for Dàdàkúàdá as long as the masses of Ilorin, even if only for linguistic and artistic reasons, continue to show great pride and patriotism as they do in projecting Dàdàkúàdá as a uniquely Ilorin masterpiece.

This chapter would look into every aspect of Dàdàkúàdá's development and examine how such development has influenced its performance characteristics.

The name and origin of Dàdàkúàdá poetry

Not one of the present artists of Dàdàkúàdá poetry is able to explain the meaning of the word Dàdàkúàdá.[2] As far as I could find, the word is neither Hausa nor Nupe. It is neither Fulani nor Gobir.[3] It is certainly not Yoruba. However, there are two possible sources to this name, and this is entirely speculative after exhausting without success any possible source for semanticity for the word.

The name "Dàdàkúàdá" could be from a kind of popular slang used at the period when the poetry was developed. This was possible, given the fact that people, especially the Yoruba people, have the habit to give names to new innovation or development in the popular culture from a current slang at the time of its creation. *Ko Sarugbo nGana*, "There-is-no-old-person-in-Ghana" (for a type of dress), *Okirika* (a name of an ethnic group in Southern Nigeria named for used clothes), Ojuku (from Ojukwu, the name of the leader of the Biafran side during the Nigerian Civil War—named for a huge size cooking pot), and the examples are limitless. This is, however, the weaker of the possibilities as there is no song whatsoever found that could help to support this speculation.

Another possible source is through the sound of the Adàmà-drum-rhythm to the songs, a kind of onomatopoeic—it was possible that the sound was (I shall use "gan" or "la" to represent a beat of the drum): "Gàn gàán gán gángàn." It is common for people, if they want to begin a song, to introduce their song with an oral beating pattern of the drum. For example, one hears, "Laalalaa lala, lalala, laa ..."

Sometimes, the lead singer in Dàdàkúàdá does this to call the drummer to change the drumming pattern. It looks plausible and believable that this second theory explains how the name "Dàdàkúàdá" comes about. In fact, the word "Dàdàkúàdá" itself shows some characteristics of a drum beating (e.g. da daa, gan gaan, kuuada, ga-an gangan). It is not new in Yoruba and indeed African culture for a musical or poetry genre or its accompanying implement to bear the name from the rhythmic beatings of its drum. For example, *Agogo* bell takes its name after its sound (i.e. "Kogo, Kogo"). Yorubas say, *Kogo, Kogo laa gbo ohun agogo*, meaning *Koko kogo* voices the bell. From this theory, one can say that the lead singer in Dàdàkúàdá performance sings, "Dàdà-kúu-àdá" to usher in a pattern of drum beating, an introductory beating, to the genre. In fact, all Dàdàkúàdá artists interviewed were unanimous in saying that the lead singer uses this pattern to introduce every performance, singing it with the following chant:

Dada-dada dadaa ku a daa oo
Un o lo lola, Ero wa sin min o
Olohun Maje n fo doo re le mooo
Dada-dada dada kua daa oo

Dada-dada dada kuadaa oo
I shall travel tomorrow, (please people, see me off in troupes!)
Oh God! I really don't want separation (from this people!)
Dada-dada da daa kuada oo.[4]

It makes much sense to me that it was from this type of performance that the name for this oral genre was originally derived.

The Dàdàkúàdá poetry is also called *Pakeke*,[5] after a kind of Sakara drum of the same name, that was introduced to Dàdàkúàdá performance at certain stage of its development. Jaigbade told me that it was simply called Pakeke by many Ilorin people because the name Dàdàkúàdá was difficult to pronounce. The Pakeke drum was introduced to Dàdàkúàdá during the periods of Ajibaye, Nnakeso, and Akanbi Eri.[6]

I collected many versions of history about how Dàdàkúàdá poetry originated. While majority of my informants seem to have agreed on a certain story, many others gave different theories of how Dàdàkúàdá originated. There are, however, occasions that I believe rightly or wrongly that I found self-contradiction in some of the narrations. I believed that Jaigbade Alao, a leading Dàdàkúàdá poet, once told me in an interview (1985) that Dàdàkúàdá originated from "Orin Eegun" (i.e. masquerade songs similar to what Oludare Olajubu has called in another work as the *iwi* songs among the Ijesa). Jaigbade I believed claimed then that when it was *Orin Eegun* or *Iwi*, poets like Afefelaye, Baba Awe, Awodi, and Abe Numo flourished.[7] What was surprising to me, however, was that later, after about two years (1987), when I contacted Jaigbade again, he denied the first story and said that Dàdàkúàdá was never associated with iwi or Orin Eegin of any kind. He claimed that the songs were independent and began on their own with Okulu as the first poet.[8] He said, however, that he did not know how or why Okulu started Dàdàkúàdá. He said further that there were various kinds of poetry then, but Okulu decided to create his own. In this later version of his story, he said that Okulu was neither a hunter nor an Egungun worshiper. After Okulu, came Abe Numo, Laomi, and Ajibaye. Jaigbade says though Ajibaye, one of these early Dàdàkúàdá poets, was (once) a worshiper of Egungun, he (Ajibaye) did not combine Dàdàkúàdá poetry performance with his Egungun outing.[9] Ajibaye's Egungun was very popular. It was called *Janduku*.[10] Ajibaye, according to Jaigbade, never took his masquerade to Dàdàkúàdá performances and that he never sang Dàdàkúàdá songs during Egungun performance. Jaigbade claimed that there were special *Orin Eegun* chanters or performers then (i.e. Baba Ilota, his [Jaigbade's] parents in Awe, etc.).[11] Jaigbade in another interview held very firm to what I believe was his second story about the origin of Dàdàkúàdá. Speaking to Jaigbade in May 2008, he was vehement about his second position to raise doubt in me as to whether or not he actually said what I believed he said about Dàdàkúàdá taking roots from Orin Egungun. Yet after I interviewed him in 1985, I felt so sure enough to prepare an article for a daily newspaper in Ilorin where I narrated that Dàdàkúàdá originated from Egungun and cited Jaigbade as my source. It seems to me that Jaigbade is in a very comfortable position in Ilorin in 2008 (he is the King of singers, as he was officially turbaned as King by the Emir of Ilorin) that he does not have to pretend to anybody about the history of his art. I also do believe that what matters to many Ilorin people in 2008 is about how the genre represents Ilorin community and not what the genre was during pre-Islamic times. I do not remember if I had taped my first discussion with Jaigbade as I would have cited his exact words when he first denied the story in 1987. Yet, his continued denial of the Egungun origin of Dàdàkúàdá has remained strong. Was it possible that I misheard him during my first interview with him in 1985!

Omoekee Amao, another prominent Dàdàkúàdá artist, claimed in an interview that Dàdàkúàdá started from *Rara* chants.[12] This type of rara chant, he said, was different from *Rara Oyo*. He called it *Rara*

Ilorin, performed by one man, one drum. Amao said that it was later developed to Dàdàkúàdá with many people introduced.[13] The intention of the development was to make the poetry further interesting and popular. Omoekee claimed that early Dàdàkúàdá groups were formed through a kind of cooperation among the artists (rara artists) who later chose a leader from among them.[14] He said that *Baalu*, the feminine form of Dàdàkúàdá performed by Ilorin women, also developed from rara. He claimed that this rara chant was still very much with Dàdàkúàdá. He said that sometimes when he went on performance, he used to stop his drummers and chanted rara.[15] I think what Omoeke was referring to was about performance technique at the inception of Dàdàkúàdá rather than about the historical origin of the genre itself. I have definitely confirmed as my research as shown, and this can be read in Chapter 4, the performance technique used at the initial stage of Dàdàkúàdá's development. This technique can be said to be similar to the most popular performance technique used in the Yoruba genre called *Rara*.

Aremu Ose, another leading Dàdàkúàdá artist, narrated another version to the origin of Dàdàkúàdá poetry. He says the original song from which Dàdàkúàdá originated was called *Tekuta*, while its artists were called *Alabada*.[16] He claimed that only Agogo (bell) was beaten to the songs back then, and that this was done by the same artist who formed the chorus group. He sang two lines from what he remembered of *Tekuta*:

Le looo, lelo mee ilo
Omama seun to o man[17]

Le loo, lelo mee ilo
Thanks indeed for knowing!

Aremu Ose claimed that modernization, that is, what the Yoruba people simply call *olaju*, brings about the development from *Tekuta* to Dàdàkúàdá. He said Laomi Alao was among the first artists who developed Dàdàkúàdá. He doesn't, however, say who the *Tekuta* artists were.[18] I found this story interesting yet difficult to accept for lack of evidence of the *Tekuta* singers and of specifically how they switched from *Tekuta* to Dàdàkúàdá. In what sense was Dàdàkúàdá modern while *Tekuta* was not?

Odolaye Aremu, alias Baba Nkwara, another "heavy weight" in Dàdàkúàdá poetry of the time of this interview, disagreed that Dàdàkúàdá originated from Rara.[19] He said that neither *Rara Oyo* nor *Rara Ilorin* was a source of Dàdàkúàdá poetry genre. He said it was God that gave Dàdàkúàdá to Ilorin. He would, however, not tell me whether any of Orin Eegun or *Tekuta* was a possible source of Dàdàkúàdá. Is it logical to say *Olohun* (God) just sent Dàdàkúàdá from heaven as he does send rain and dew to the earth? I personally do not think Odolaye was serious when he told me that!

I personally believe that this poetry genre must have been a gradual development from a proto cultural song and performance. I was not helped much through my interviews of many Ilorin people who were generally passionate about Dàdàkúàdá or even people who were less so. It was interesting though that many fans interviewed believed that *Orin Eegun* could be the source of Dàdàkúàdá, even though some Dàdàkúàdá artists disagreed with this belief![20]

I have chosen *Iwi* as a similar genre to the possible original poetic genre from which Dàdàkúàdá started because after reading Oludare Ojaide's work on Egungun, I found out that some characteristic features of Dàdàkúàdá are very similar to that of *Iwi*, the Egungun poetry among Ijesa people, which Olajubu described very elaborately.[21] In a M.A. thesis he did for the University of Lagos, Olajubu enumerates the characteristics of Iwi.[22] My findings so far in this research on Dàdàkúàdá performance enable me to view the two genres to have striking similarities and even possibly a father and child relationship. However, Ilorin history does not show that Ijesa people particularly migrated to the place now called Ilorin in any significant number, nor whether Ijesa Iwi performers took their performances to Ilorin before Islam was institutionalized in the area. My new thinking, therefore, is that perhaps the similarity that *Iwi Egungun* has with Dàdàkúàdá was only accidental or, at best, came from the general similarity of some features that Yoruba traditional genres share.

Yet, if the Ijesa migration did not happen and Dàdàkúàdá has no direct link to Iwi, it is not entirely impossible for Egungun to have important connection to the origin of Dàdàkúàdá. As I presented in a scholarly paper and recently reproduced in my book, *African Discourse in Islam, Oral Traditions and Performance*, the ancestral origin of Egungun is actually nearer Ilorin than most other present-day Yoruba lands. I will repeat some of my arguments on that issue here to ensure clarity for the reader of this material. However, more can be obtained from the relevant chapter ("Yoruba Egungun: Some Critical Thoughts") in the *African Discourse* book. Reverend Samuel Johnson had said that Egungun originated from Nupe land.[23] A large portion of Kwara State that Ilorin currently serves as headquarters and capital city is a Nupe land, so Nupe's culture is bound to continue to have some influences on Ilorin. Also, I have explained in the introductory chapter of this book that Nupe people were among the inhabitants or indigenes of the present-day Ilorin.

Some of the characteristic features of Iwi performance that are also found in Dàdàkúàdá are the "dialogue technique" and "the call and response technique." In fact, the dialogue was the main feature of Dàdàkúàdá performance at an early stage of its development. Some lines in the dialogue technique of Iwi poetry as given by Olajubu are:

LASUN: Nitori a won ba baa mi ni
ADISA: Ooto ni, bee naa ni
LASUN: Onimogun, mo oro toromi lowo aje
ADISA: Omo Eji gbojo ni o maape nigba gbogbo

LASUN: It is for my father's sake
ADISA: It is true and perfectly so
LASUN: Onimogun, son of riches who greases my palm with money
ADISA: You must hail offspring of Ejigbojo always[24]

Some lines in "The call and response style" given by Olajubu are:

LASUN: Iba o
     Eje n riba ki to sere

ELEGBE: Iba o,
     Eje n riba ki n to sere

LASUN: Niteri awon babaa mi
     Onimogun, mo ore, to'ro mi lowo ajo

ELEGBE: I ba o
     Eje n riba kin to sere[25]

LASUN: Homage
     Let me pay homage before I start my play

CHORUS: Homage
     Let me pay homage before I start my play

LASUN: It is all for my father's sake, Onimogun, son of riches who greases my
     Palm with money

CHORUS: Homage,
     Let me pay homage before I start my play.

There is no difference between the above two techniques and the dialogue and the leader and *Omomose* (chorus) techniques of Dàdàkúàdá performance. Yet the two reasons, that is, the Nupe's nearestness or nativity to Ilorin and the similarity of Dàdàkúàdá to *Iwi* Egungun, may not be enough to conclude with certainty that Dàdàkúàdá started from *Orin Egungun*. What might be safe to infer was that the Egungun songs and performances have important influence on Dàdàkúàdá.

The Dàdàkúàdá artists and stages of Dàdàkúàdá's development

One cannot talk of the stages of Dàdàkúàdá poetry's development without mentioning the artists who performed the poetry genre from the earliest time. It is around them that everything about Dàdàkúàdá revolved and developed.

The first stage of its development was the stage identified as the birth of the poetry. Okulu is identified as the first Dàdàkúàdá poet.[26] This stage only involved very few artists: Okulu, the oral poet, and a drummer who accompanied him.[27] No one remembers the exact mode of the songs they sang.[28] The *Gangan* drum was the only drum used at this stage.[29]

The second stage developed during Abenumo's time. There were few changes from the first stage of Okulu to the second stage of Abenumo. The changes consisted of the number of drummers and poets performing together at a particular venue. About two to three people sang simultaneously while two, three, or four people accompanied them with drum.[30] The songs in this stage were said to be similar to those of the first stage. Only *Gangan* drum was also used here.[31]

The third stage of Dàdàkúàdá's development was the period of Ajibaye and Laomi. Dàdàkúàdá became enormously popular during this stage. It was said to have reached its peak.[32] It was said that any ceremony in Ilorin then without Ajibaye's performance was looked down upon. Such a ceremony was regarded as that which *Ko lese nle*, "had no leg on the ground."[33] Ajibaye was said to be very talented. A fan said when Ajibaye sang, a person could dance himself to death![34] It was during this stage that *Pakeke* drum was introduced to Dàdàkúàdá.[35] *Pakeke* is a one-sided, small, rounded drum. This is used together with *gangan* to supply sound to Dàdàkúàdá. It was from this stage that this poetry also came to be known as *Pakeke*.[36] The number of drums used in this stage increased to about six.[37] Also, the dialogue style was the main feature of performance at this stage. Ajibaye was, however, more popular than any singer in Ilorin.[38] It was said that Dàdàkúàdá, during this stage, suppressed all other Ilorin social-religious[39] poetry. It was during this period that a person (or persons) was separated for chorusing purposes and named *Omomose*, while another person bore the name *Oga*, the leader.[40] In other words, *Omomose*, which literally meant "the pupil is perfect," was the name used for the person heading the chorus group or the entire chorus group itself. The person leading the chorus group was usually the most senior in the chorus group and was also the second-in-command of the Dàdàkúàdá group. It can be said without mincing words that the third stage was, therefore, a marking point in the development of Dàdàkúàdá.

Ajibaye could also be known as the hero of the third stage. He brought Dàdàkúàdá to the limelight. Jaigbade told me, "Ajibaye brightened it (Dàdàkúàdá). He washed it clean."[41] Other Dàdàkúàdá poets during this stage were Inakeso, Akanbi Eri, Mamadu Aro (who learned it from Laomi), Akanho Ogo, Ajadi Okan, and Amuda Pele, a younger brother to Laomi.[42] Apart from the *Pakeke* drum, other drums used then were *Iyalu, Gangan, Emele, Atona,* and *Aropo*.[43] Among notable drummers of Ajibaye were Alabi Oge, Adesina, and Amao Eruda.[44]

The fourth stage of Dàdàkúàdá's development is the present-day stage, the modern or globalized stage, depending on what or how one wants to describe it. It probably started from about 1940 and continued till date, even after many of the notable performers and stars of the stage have passed to the world beyond. Many of the major performers of this stage who are still alive: Jaigbade, Saka Kolobo, Olanrewaju Oloje, and more. I described this stage a globalization state because although the stage started in the 1940s (more later about 1940 as the date when the present leading Dàdàkúàdá poet—Jaigbade—came into the genre under the tutelage of his master Akanho Elefunde in Olooru, Ilorin Emirate), yet its longevity has enabled it to witness dramatic influences in the contemporary Electronic Age. However, perhaps the most important reason for assessing Dàdàkúàdá in 2018 and beyond as still belonging to the fourth stage was because the King of Dàdàkúàdá, Jaigbade Alao, who led Dàdàkúàdá from the beginning of this stage in the 1940s is very much alive in 2018 and still performing Dàdàkúàdá with zeal and passion even as new performers continue to join.

A lot of innovations have been made in Dàdàkúàdá poetry genre in the fourth stage. The first important change is that Dàdàkúàdá is rendered more as songs and music (lyrics) in the fourth stage.[45] Modern instruments like microphones and speakers are now in use. Jaigbade Jimoh Alao, highly regarded within Ilorin land as the present-day leader of Dàdàkúàdá poets in Ilorin, says he came into Dàdàkúàdá poetry on 5 January 1940. Jaigbade had been an Agbe artist, like his parents, before then. Odolaye Aremu, another "heavy weight" of Dàdàkúàdá poetry (who is more popular in other Yoruba lands), could not remember the exact time he started. He also would not say which Emir was on the throne in Ilorin at his commencement—all he said was that there had been Dàdàkúàdá before he started singing. No one taught him. He was only interested and, therefore, decided to establish his own group. This was unlike Jaigbade who went on an apprenticeship under a leader. It is popularly believed, however, that both Odolaye and Jaigbade Alao started about the same time. In short, the third stage of Dàdàkúàdá's development must have taken place sometime between the late 1890s and the beginning of the 1940s.

Aremu Ose is another popular Dàdàkúàdá artist. He had many things in common with Jaigbade. He claimed that he learnt Dàdàkúàdá art from Akanho Ogo of Oloru, Ajadi Okan of Abemi, and Amuda Pele of Ile Ogo—all in Ilorin. Amuda Pele is said to be a younger brother to Laomi. Both Aremu Ose and Jaigbade Alao were together in apprenticeship, probably with Ajadi Okan. Omoekee Amao, a former pupil of Jaigbade Alao, was also a very popular Dàdàkúàdá poet. He claimed to have graduated and started his independent Dàdàkúàdá group in 1953. He was in apprenticeship for nine years. Other Dàdàkúàdá poets in the fourth stage are Lanrewaju Oloje, Saka Aremu Kolobo, Obe Lawo, Karimu Isale Abata, Alabi Olowawa, Amode Amori, Ramani Orelope, Aiyegbajeje Akanbi, Alhaji Jolomiro, Anafi Alao, Baba Eyin Oke Ajape, Oba Ode, and many other less popular ones.

Many new innovations were introduced to Dàdàkúàdá during this stage. Many Dàdàkúàdá artists now used microphones and speakers. Omoekee Amao claimed to be the first artist to introduce and to launch the microphonic instruments, which he bought for *Ogota apo ati apo merin*, "about 64.00 naira—Nigerian currency" in the 1950s! When he first used the instrument in Ilorin, Dàdàkúàdá fans and the Ilorin public reacted negatively. Most of the fans stopped patronizing him, questioning the morale behind the *domgburu*m oversized-thing, he now sang for them through. However, people gradually became used to it and started inviting him to ceremonies as before. This, according to Omoekee, was around 1957.

Other innovations to the Dàdàkúàdá poetry were in the addition of *Akuba* drum into the drums to Dàdàkúàdá. The *Akuba* was a kind of Hausa drum, which was hardly used by the Yoruba before then. An important innovation at the fourth stage was also the introduction of *Boto*. This is a kind of messenger who the members of the audience send to the artist (or the lead vocalist). The role of Boto is fully discussed under "Performance Technique" in a succeeding chapter. Even though the system of lead-follow or lead-chorus (i.e., *Oga—Omomose)* was fully introduced during Ajibaye's era. It is at the present stage that the chorus group was enlarged, comprising of as many as eight members. Also, the number of members of the drumming group was increased with the addition of Akuba and Sekere. It is the present set of Dàdàkúàdá artists that started producing records (popularly called as "plate" among the fans), initially on records and now on CDs and DVDs. Odolaye Aremu was the first to wax record in the mid-1940s. Ten years after his first record, no other Dàdàkúàdá poet had brought out a record/plate. Presently, all the modern Dàdàkúàdá poets have many records to their credit. Jaigbade alone has as many as over 50 records/DVDs to his credit. These records/DVDs are sold in recording studios and musical shops throughout Nigeria. Before he died in 1997, Odolaye was said to have far more than 50 records. However, when asked during an interview, neither he nor any available documentation readily shows the number of records to his credit.

Dàdàkúàdá poetry is not a family, household, or ancestrally inherited poetry genre as is the case with many traditional African traditional poetry genres.[46] Family or household genre in the African sense is often the traditional performance that is carried from family to family often because of its spiritual dimensions or professional or cultural link to family. Most of the past and present Dàdàkúàdá poets came into it due to their personal interest and not because of family reasons. In the traditional art,[47] this means that Dàdàkúàdá is not carried from a generation to another generation within a single family. I have not come across any history of Dàdàkúàdá artists that show that their parents or ancestors had been Dàdàkúàdá artists themselves. Dàdàkúàdá artists can be found from different parts of Ilorin and are mostly males.[48] Majority of them, however, come from *Oko Ilorin*, the Ilorin villages, although many have settled in the Ilorin city. As I have discussed in the brief history of Ilorin, the Ilorin city is usually referred to as *Ile Ilorin*. This expression is heard mainly from Ilorin indigenes.

Dàdàkúàdá versus other Ilorin poetry

There are many other traditional poetry genres in Ilorin apart from Dàdàkúàdá. Some of these poetry genres have been there before the evolution of Dàdàkúàdá, and some were recently developed. The generality of Ilorin poetry have already been briefly explained in my introductory chapter. I classify all of them into (1) pre-Islamic arts and (2) post-Islamic arts. Another classification one can give to Ilorin oral arts is (1) religious oral poetry and (2) nonreligious oral poetry. The development of Dàdàkúàdá has a lot of impact on other traditional poetry of Ilorin. Before Dàdàkúàdá, *Agbe* and *Sekere* oral arts flourished in Ilorin.[49] However, the popularity of Dàdàkúàdá has suppressed these other genres of poetry. The hitherto fans of *Agbe* and *Sekere* artists seemed to have abandoned their arts for Dàdàkúàdá.[50] Many reasons could be responsible for the emergence of Dàdàkúàdá as the preferred and widely prevalent traditional oral art performance in Ilorin: First, the charm and popularity of the lead Dàdàkúàdá singer at any given time, and second, the fact that Dàdàkúàdá remained uniquely known as Ilorin art instead of Agbe and Sakara which are equally indigenous to several other Yoruba communities. The oral traditions about Ajibaye, an ancient Dàdàkúàdá artist, indicated that he held community to his performance by the share power of his charm. He was also greatly talented, and his name spread like wild fire across Ilorin land. It seemed easy for him to displace other artists and for his genre to displace other genres in Ilorin people's hearts.

Another unique feature of Dàdàkúàdá was the introduction of new drums such as Akuba, which was done by Jaigbade, and the chorus group, which traditions indicated was done by Ajibaye. Also, the many innovative performance techniques all combine to make Dàdàkúàdá the darling poetry in Ilorin. It might also be said that the nature of Ilorin community as the city that attracted immigrants, Yoruba hunters, traders who come to Ilorin markets, or who passed through Ilorin because of its geographic location as the gateway between the north and the south cities must have continued to providing the right timing for the emergence of Dàdàkúàdá as the uniquely Ilorin art. It is little wonder, therefore, that the Ilorin indigenes are proud of Dàdàkúàdá and easily identify with it as they found something they could show to their guests, especially Yoruba people from other Yoruba communities in Nigeria and abroad, as a uniquely Ilorin art. Describing this situation, an elderly woman I interviewed who has remained a fan of Dàdàkúàdá throughout her life said the time was right for the emergence of Dàdàkúàdá.[51]

From the period of Ajibaye when Dàdàkúàdá reached its peak, both *Agbe* and *Sekere* arts started a downward turn. In this twenty-first-century Ilorin, one hardly hears *Sekere* and *Agbe* arts or sees their artists in any significant numbers in Ilorin. Other poetry genres that were introduced to Ilorin after Dàdàkúàdá (i.e. *Were* and *Nolo*) have been greatly influenced by Dàdàkúàdá. Many Dàdàkúàdá songs or poetry and performance patterns are adopted in *Were*.[52] Even the *Bembe* art adopts Dàdàkúàdá songs. Only those I would describe as pure Islamic genres like *Waka*, *Bandiri*, and *Orin Makondoro* do not imitate Dàdàkúàdá songs. The Islamic genres maintain uniquely religious songs and themes. I am sure the explanation for this is that those songs or poetry are still a 100% reflection of Islamic history and messages. Their composers and performers make extra effort to ensure that they do not imitate a popular traditional African oral genre, which they think would compromise their Islamic status or sensibility. For *Bandiri* is rendered only in Arabic language and the drums and drumming patterns are imitated from similar Muslim cultures in North Africa and perhaps across the Islamic world.

What might surprise (or not surprise) many readers is that I actually feel very strongly that in the contemporary stage of Dàdàkúàdá's development (i.e. the fourth stage), Dàdàkúàdá poetry genre might take a downward trend in popularity within Ilorin! This might still happen even though Dàdàkúàdá is growing popular like a wild fire across other areas of the Yoruba land, from Ibadan to Lagos and to Abeokuta and the Ijebu Ode and Ijebu Igbo. Islam continues to attain new strengths in Ilorin, and new global traditions of television and electronic performances seem to be engaging Ilorin youths away from Dàdàkúàdá. It is an irony that people across other Yoruba towns and cities seem to enjoy it (and not necessarily prouder of Dàdàkúàdá) than those from its Ilorin home. It may also be said that for people from across other Yoruba lands, their reasons for patronizing Dàdàkúàdá could be because of their search for an authentic Yoruba performance genre, which retains its local flavor and idiosyncrasies. The truth is that the globalization forces and the new electronic cultures have drastically affected all areas of Yoruba land, and Dàdàkúàdá presents, for some Yoruba people, oral poetry, songs, and voices that remind them of indigenous Yoruba poetic dialects and characteristics. This does not mean that Dàdàkúàdá does not suffer its own conflicts due to the ferocity of the intrusion of the global forces and the declining cultural artistic tastes among the Ilorin people (see *Globalization, Oral Performance, and African Traditional Poetry*).

However, it seems that Dàdàkúàdá has done much better than many other Yoruba oral arts in retaining many of its original outlooks, including local voice and singing patterns. I have heard some non-Ilorin people laughed with joy and confessed to have enjoyed simply listening to native Ilorin dialect and would not be surprised if similar feelings and reactions are generated when those people listen to Dàdàkúàdá poetry itself. As presented, Dàdàkúàdá is performed in pure Ilorin dialect of the Yoruba with stronger Arabic and Hausa/Fulani inflections and Islamic cultural influences. Apart from the elderly people who still patronize the poetry genre, unfortunately Dàdàkúàdá is becoming less and less popular with youths and social groups in the global-century Ilorin. The Ilorin *Sanmari* (youths) prefer *Fuji* and Hip-hop to Dàdàkúàdá performance in their ceremonies.[53] It must be said, however, that the attitude of youths to Dàdàkúàdá in villages and rural areas surrounding Ilorin is not the same as what obtains in the Ilorin city and cosmopolitan metropolis. Nevertheless, Dàdàkúàdá poets are still sustained more because they receive invitations from outside Ilorin Emirate and especially from outside Kwara State. Jaigbade told me that he had an average of one performance outside Ilorin (both within and outside Kwara) to Ilorin's two to three performances per week.[54] Omoekee Amao also claimed the same.[55] Odolaye Aremu, however, said almost all his performances were outside Ilorin community in Oyo, Ibadan, and Abeokuta areas.[56] Aremu Ose and Saka Kolobo have their major performances within Ilorin land. In Ilorin, the oral artists generally record their maximum performances during the specific months in which the Ilorin people conduct most of their wedding ceremonies. These months are *Safar* (i.e. the month following *Muaram*, the first month of the Islamic calendar), *Nabiyu* (the month in which Prophet Mohammad was born—Rabiyyu'l Awal), and *Isimi Awe* (the preparatory month to *Ramadan*, *Ramadan* is the month in which adult Muslims are required to fast for 29 or 30 compulsory days—called *Al Shaban*).[57] These three months, *Safar, Nabiyu, and Isimi Awe (Al-Shaban)*, are usually slated by Ilorin people for *Nikkah* (weddings).

During a *Nabiyu* that fell around November to December 1987, I went round major parts of Ilorin to see which artists were performing during weekend parties. Of the 28 places I visited, Dàdàkúàdá artists were performing only in ten. Ere Baalu was in four places. All the remaining places had young Fuji artists. In other words, Dàdàkúàdá recorded approximately 36% of the total percentage of the arts found performing evan at that time. This trend is not peculiar to Dàdàkúàdá alone. As can be seen, neither *Molo, Sekere,* nor Agbe artists were seen performing. It was true, like Jaigbade also observed during an interview I had with him around the time, that the older generation or senior people still preferred Dàdàkúàdá poetry in Ilorin,[58] but it was also certain that the youths who were the ones that mostly wed do not share the sentiment of the elderly people in the community when it comes to Dàdàkúàdá. However, it is the youths who enjoyed the kind of grand ceremonies that marked naming and birthday celebrations. The twenty-first-century

Ilorin is even now showing new trends where Police Bands are being hired to perform at wedding ceremonies. This action of engaging the Police Band is totally new and has no precedence in Ilorin cultural behavior. I repeated my survey in May 2008 of the Ilorin traditional arts performing in Ilorin evenings, and the Dàdàkúàdá data fell significantly and so was the Fuji data. However, it must be noted that May 2008 did not fall on any of the traditional wedding months in Ilorin.

Yet, within Ilorin, nonreligious indigenous poetry that includes Dàdàkúàdá, *Were*, *Molo*, *Agbe*, *Sekere*, *Asa*, and *Bembe*, Dàdàkúàdá is still the most popular among the Ilorin people. *Fuji*, which developed from *Were*, and which I discovered was loved mostly by many youths cannot be said to be an indigenous poetry of Ilorin. While it is true that the Proto form of *Fuji* (i.e. *Were*) started and spread to all Yoruba lands from Ilorin,[59] the later metamorphosis of *Were* into *Fuji* did not take place in Ilorin.[60] This origin story alone is enough to show that *Fuji* is not an Ilorin traditional poetry, even though *Were* is. It might, therefore, seem an irony, in the sense that whereas Dàdàkúàdá's popularity spread like a wild fire among Yoruba in the southwestern part of Nigeria, it was *Fuji* that continued to attain this fit among the Ilorin youths from late twentieth century into the early twenty-first century! *Ere Baalu*, a twin sister of Dàdàkúàdá, is also popular. Its popularity, as can be seen from above analysis, is below that of Dàdàkúàdá. *Agbe* also fares well. The *Agbe* artists perform mostly during the day in naming or even wedding ceremonies. There are, therefore, still *Agbe artists* in Ilorin. The *Sekere* group still exists also, but very few *Sekere* artists can be seen performing within Ilorin. The *Bembe* and *Kakaki* groups are also in the twenty-first-century Ilorin. They don't usually perform in the nights. Of all the nonreligious (non-Islamic) arts, Dàdàkúàdá has the widest acceptance in Ilorin. Yet, its popularity, like I already mentioned, is taking a downward trend within Ilorin even as it is assuming an upward trend in other Yoruba communities in Nigeria. Dàdàkúàdá is falling from the peak position that it had reached in the third stage of its development.

Dàdàkúàdá, when compared with the religious (Islamic) poetry of Ilorin, is decidedly not the most popular. Chanting of the Holy Quran, for example, is the most common of all artistic activities in Ilorin. In almost every house, nook and corner, one activity or another relating to the Quran recitation is taking place.

Another Islamic oral art performance is the *Waka*. This is equally highly favored, in terms of social engagement, to Dàdàkúàdá in the Ilorin metropolis. *Waka* has been explained in Chapter 2 and discussed extensively in my *Cultural Plurality* book. The group *Waka*, as already pointed out, is employed on every eve of Wolimat day. Ilorin traditional wedding rituals that include *Wolimat* (ceremony marking the completion of the learning of the Holy Quran) start from Tuesdays and end on Saturdays or Sundays—a total of six days at most! Majority of Ilorin families have recently reduced this to a weekend ceremony. Since every Ilorin child, by convention and tradition, is expected to attend local Quranic school, such ceremony is quite rampant in Ilorin. Completion of the 60 chapters of the Quran is at first marked with low-keyed ceremony—like killing of fowls for food. But the ceremony with pomp and pageantry is postponed and later marked with the wedding ceremony of the pupils. A cow is often killed on such occasion for food. Actually, both the bride and bridegroom celebrate Wolimat on the same day, in the same way.[61]

There are, however, some Quranic school dropouts who don't do Wolimat. These are not more than 5% at most in the Ilorin community. A person can celebrate a grand Wolimat only once, most often when taking his first wife. If he later marries more wives either as taking to polygamy or as a result of a divorce or death, no Wolimat is celebrated by him. The bride (or groom) is allowed to celebrate their own Wolimat if they have not done so before. Because of convenience, there have been cases of Ilorin youths that have done their grand Wolimat (as part of a mass Wolimat ceremony in a household for example), but this number is very small indeed.

So in every marriage session, there are about 95% Wolimat celebrations, and in every Wolimat, a group *Waka* art is invited. The *Waka* groups are always very engaged throughout marriage sessions. In fact, on a Wolimat Eve, a group is usually booked for about six performances. It may move from one place to another, starting at about 11:00 p.m. and spending approximately one hour in every performance. There is no alternative to the *Waka* group performance at a Wolimat Eve in Ilorin. It is an institutionalized tradition. This is very much unlike the marriage ceremonies grand parties where the celebrant has a choice of calling from *Were, Fuji, Agbe, Sekere,* Dàdàkúàdá, and *Baalu.* It has already been said that Fuji is highly favored by the youths than Dàdàkúàdá. That shows clearly that *Waka* is more engaged than Dàdàkúàdá. As for the Ilorin housewives' Waka, there is no ceremony where it is not sung or performed in Ilorin: marriage, burial (only of very elderly departees), naming ceremonies, and more. The one-man Waka poetry is performed more than Dàdàkúàdá. *Orin Makondoro* is exclusively performed during ceremonies—Wolimat, marriage, naming of members (students and Mallams), and so on of the Makondoro Islamic schools. The chants of the Islamic Mallams are only done during Islamic preaching and discussions.

From the above and despite what seems a contradiction about its status when compared with other Ilorin traditional poetry genres, it can be clearly seen that Dàdàkúàdá is the most important and most popular of what I call Ilorin indigenous nonreligious songs or poetry; however, Dàdàkúàdá is still thrown far behind when we consider the Islamic poetry genres in Ilorin.

Notes

1 Therefore, any seeming repetition is hereby acknowledged.
2 All the Dàdàkúàdá artists interviewed confessed to the fact that they themselves could not explain the meaning of Dàdàkúàdá.
3 Nobody from the speakers of those languages (among those interviewed) could give the meaning of the word. They all said it was not a word in their languages.
4 Personal interview with Jimoh Jaigbade Alao, 9 August 1987.
5 Personal interview with Omoekee Amao, 8 August 1987.
6 Personal interview with Aremu Ose, 9 August 1987.
7 In an earlier interview conducted by me in October 1985, he told me that it originated from Orin Egungun. This information was depended upon in my article published in *The Herald* of Tuesday (5 November 1987): 8, titled "Dàdàkúàdá: The Music of Ilorin."
8 Personal interview with Jimoh Jaigbade Alao, 9 August 1987.
9 It is very difficult to accept some of his explanations on this. I believe very strongly that Okulu and other people mentioned were either hunters or Egungun worshipers. Going by the historical origin of Ilorin (as explained in the introductory chapter), one will see that these were the major two traditional activities in Ilorin at the onset. I also realized in the interview that Jaigbade was trying to erase anything that had to do with Egungun from Dàdàkúàdá. This is understandable given the present-day religious value of Ilorin people. It is possible that Jaigbade does that to "wash clean" and safe his poetry from what he himself calls "intensive attacks" from religious leaders in Ilorin. In fact, when he said Ajibaye, a one-time very popular Dàdàkúàdá artist, was an Egungun worshiper, he quickly added that Ajibaye had been greatly Islamised and was an Islamic Mallam before his death. My other findings, however, reveal otherwise. Saara Odee, a woman over 75 years old, told me that Ajibaye, though he went to Mecca, never stopped worshipping Egungun until his death.
10 Personal interview with Jimoh Jaigbade Alao, 9 August 1987.
11 Ibid.
12 Personal interview with Omoekee Amao, 8 August 1987.
13 Though his claim differs from Jaigbade's, the latter's claim can be relied upon since he taught Omoekee Dàdàkúàdá art.
14 Personal interview with Omoekee Amao, 8 August 1987.
15 Ibid., Saka Kolobo and many other Dàdàkúàdá artists also claim the same thing. Saka says he chants *rara* during Dàdàkúàdá performance. He, however, does not say *rara* is the source of Dàdàkúàdá poetry. This comes from *Osaro Sunday*. Prod. Bayo Alayande, Radio Kwara, 25 October 1987.

16 Personal interview with Aremu Ose, 26 August 1987.
17 Ibid.
18 Ibid.
19 Personal interview with Odolaye Aremu, 12 August 1987.
20 I conducted many interviews with many fans of Dàdàkúàdá poetry in Ilorin. Some of these are recorded on tape (audio cassette) between July 1987 and January 1988.
21 Among these characteristics include performance technique. This and others shall be fully discussed as we progress.
22 I.O. Olajubu, "Iwi: Egungun Chants in Yoruba Oral Literature," M.A. Thesis, U of Lagos (1970).
23 J. Samuel, *The History of the Yorubas.* Ed. Dr. O. Johnson (Lagos, CMS (Lagos) Bookshop, 1960): 160.
24 Ibid., 95.
25 Ibid., 101.
26 Personal interview with Jimoh Jiagbade Alao, 9 August 1987.
27 Ibid.
28 All the artists and the fans I interviewed cannot recollect. There is also no available recording of his songs.
29 Personal interview with Jimoh Jaigbade Alao, 9 August 1987.
30 Ibid.
31 Ibid.
32 Ibid.
33 Ibid.
34 Personal interviews with Saaratu Odee, 2 September 1987.
35 Personal interviews with Omoekee Amao, 8 August 1987, and Jaigbade Alao, 9 August 1987.
36 Ibid.
37 Ibid.
38 Ibid., this is also expressed by all the Dàdàkúàdá fans interviewed.
39 Nonreligious poetry is used here to refer to all those Ilorin indigenous poetry that are not essentially meant for religious purposes: those poetry which are always accused and condemned by the Muslim preachers as un-Islamic. More explanation shall come later on this.
40 Personal interview with Jimoh Jaigbade Alao, 9 August 1987.
41 Ibid.
42 Personal interview with Aremu Ose, 26 August 1987.
43 Personal interview with Jimoh Jaigbade Alao, 9 August 1987.
44 Ibid., also with Aremu Ose, 26 August 1987.
45 It is popularly called and categorized in the present day as Dàdàkúàdá music.
46 That is the generalized consensus in Ilorin—among the fans. Odolaye Aremu who is also popular and could have been an alternate candidate for leadership is hardly patronized in Ilorin. Ninety percent of the fans interviewed says of odolaye "E le ke eebu ni," that is, "his mouth is full of abuses." He is also soon mainly as a political poet. Adebayo Alayande, then principal controller of Yoruba Program on Radio Kwara, Ilorin, says,

> Within Ilorin indigines, people who like Dàdàkúàdá will prefer Jaigbade. He knows Oriki, he's slower ...

Adebayo rightly observes that some people even think that Jaigbade is the originator of Dàdàkúàdá poetry—personal interview with Adebayo Alayande, 3 September 1987. One interesting thing, however, is that when you mention Dàdàkúàdá to Yorubas in Oyo, Lagos, Ogun, and Ondo, Odolaye Aremu is the artist that readily comes to their mind—most students who come from these areas that I spoke to say they only knew Odolaye Aremu.

47 Personal interview with Jimoh Jaigbade Alao, 9 August 1987.

48 The female's music, a sister poetry to Dàdàkúàdá, is known as Baalu. It is thoroughly discussed under literature review.

49 All artists and fans interviewed attest to that.

50 Most of the present Dàdàkúàdá poets had hitherto been either *Agbe* or *Sekere* poets.

51 Personal interview with Saaratu Odee, 2 September 1987.

52 In fact, because of this fact, Odolaye Aremu during an interview, on 8 December 1987, claims that he regards most of the modern-day Yoruba oral artists as his pupils—since virtually all of them sing from his own self-composed songs.

53 This shall be proved as we proceed on in the chapter.

54 Personal interview with Jimoh Jaigbade Alao, 24 September 1987.

55 Personal interview with Omoekee Amao, 24 August 1987.

56 Personal interview with Odolaye Aremu, 12 August 1987. Also, all fans interviewed attest to that.

57 Abdul Razaq Abdullahi, undergraduate, B.A. Arabic University of Ilorin (he helped when I was calculating and identifying the Islamic months concerned).

58 Personal interview with Jimoh Jaigbade Alao, 9 August 1987. I also observed this during my visits to their field performances, including those I recorded on tape (audio cassette).

59 A. Na'Allah, "Arabic and Islamic Education in Ilorin," in *Unilorin Pedagogue, Journal of Education Students Association,* University of Ilorin (1985): 37; see also "Oral and Performantic Arts of Ilorin," *The Herald* (8 September 1987): 9+; and M.A. Omibiyi Obidike, "Islam Influence on Yoruba Music," in *Africa Notes,* VIII.2 (1981): 45–47.

60 It is believed that this took place in Ibadan and Lagos areas.

61 I attended local Quranic schools myself and participated in the Wolimat celebrations of many schoolmates. I planned to also celebrate my own Wolimat during my marriage ceremony, by the grace of God.

4   Influence of Islam on Dàdàkúàdá

It has already been established from the preceding chapters that Islam in Ilorin has very strong influence on the totality of the lives of the people and the culture of Ilorin. Even without a separate chapter focusing on Islam's influence on Dàdàkúàdá, almost every topic in this book already shows its important relationship to Islam or to Islamic issues: the history of Ilorin, various poetry performances in Ilorin, the origin of Dàdàkúàdá, the developmental stages of Dàdàkúàdá, its performance techniques, and more. In short, on almost every stage of this work, on almost every page, evidences of Islam's influence on Dàdàkúàdá are glaring.

First, and any one may want to ask, that if it is actually true that Dàdàkúàdá genre started from Egungun or has a close relationship with Egungun worship or worshipers at the time of its initial development, why is it then that there is no element of Egungun songs in the present-day Dàdàkúàdá poetry?[1] It is extremely difficult at the first hearing to relate Dàdàkúàdá to Egungun. Yet, it is precisely due to the fact that Egungun is rooted in ancestral worship and thus contradicts a basic tenant of Islam that would easily explain why Dàdàkúàdá genre in a contemporary Muslim community would not show any direct element of Egungun worship. It takes a person who has been aware of the historical background of the poetry to relate Dàdàkúàdá to Egungun.

In the contemporary performance of Dàdàkúàdá, an *Iba*—homage (the opening of the performance on a performance field, for example) is first paid to Allah—usually in recitation of Quranic verses—at the introductory stage of Dàdàkúàdá performance (see Chapter 5).[2] Even during the middle stage of performance, the Dàdàkúàdá artists always recite a number of Quranic verses in their original Arabic language. They use moral or religious lessons in the Quran or other Islamic sources to shape some of their poetry.

What is very interesting of most of Dàdàkúàdá artists in contemporary Ilorin, as Jaigbade himself confirmed to me, they have Quranic scholars who teach them the Quran and the Hadith.[3] Many of the Dàdàkúàdá artists are well versed in the Quran. Even where any of them cannot read or write the Arabic language, they memorize the Quran and are able to recite the verses from head as part of their performance. Their knowledge of the Quran and the Hadith is absolutely evident in the kind of moral teachings contained in their songs and the way those songs are sometime presented. Although rather uncommon, it is not new to hear Dàdàkúàdá songs that resemble Waka performance in the ways they praise the Prophet of Islam, Mohammed. In one case, even in direct textual imitation of the Waka songs that are called *Madiu Annabi*—that is, song for praising and praying for the Prophet of Islam!

In addition, it is observed that contemporary Dàdàkúàdá artists have guarded against utterances that are regarded in Islam as *Alfasha* or foul talks. Jaigbade told me that during Ajibaye and other past Dàdàkúàdá poets' periods, all kinds of talks were freely used in the poetry, without cause for shame.[4] In my discussions with Saka Kolobo in March 2007, he remembered as a child the heavy doses of blunt songs that the Dàdàkúàdá singer would feed to his audience on a performance field and the kind of intoxicated responses that could be expected from such audience. Contemporary Dàdàkúàdá poets, however, try as much as possible to live up to the standard of the highly Islamized community to which they now belong.

The moral standard on the field of performance is high. Alcoholic drinks are not usually allowed, especially when Dàdàkúàdá artists are performing within Ilorin land.[5] It is a big deal when a non-Islamic (or non-Christian) performing art group avoids alcoholic drinks during social events in Nigeria. Alcohol is usually among the first of what Nigerian performing artists expect the celebrant to provide to them, and most celebrants knew that they better get strong alcohol ready if they want the singers to be happy and to perform well and if they want the event to be "groovy." This may be a tradition that was carried over from traditional African culture such as the Yoruba culture in which the celebrant makes sure that *Emu* or *Oguro*, both local wines, is not too far from the social singer if he or she wants it.

The Ilorin Dàdàkúàdá poets are also strict about people they perform for. They always make sure, according to Jaigbade and Aremu Ose, that such patrons would not corrupt their performance morally, religiously, and socially. I am still trying to figure out what these artists consider as "moral, religious and social" corruption or any other thing capable of corrupting their performance. Perhaps, an interesting question would be how seriously do they carry out this vetting? It seems to me that their reason for vetting people who invite them to perform may be more to demonstrate their sensitivity to Islam than concern about any real corruption of their performance. Although the poets would readily and strongly speak about their comportment to what they believe the Ilorin Muslims regard as Islamic ethics at home and in their performance fields, it is difficult to know how well they observe this strategy of conforming to the moral standard of the Islamic Ilorin. I personally believe that although most Dàdàkúàdá artists would claim that they are devout Muslims who observe Islamic ethics on performance field, it is better said than done.

I know for certain that Jaigbade Alao performs his Muslim *salat* very effortlessly having observed him perform salat in the late 1980s and having later prayed with him at a congregation in 2008! Yet, it is difficult to know whether the generality of the Dàdàkúàdá artists believe what they say regarding this Islamic moral standard to be true, or whether they say them only to embrace Ilorin Islamic hegemony and protect themselves from critical comments and public rebuke by Ilorin Islamic scholars. I personally attended public performances by Jaigbade and Aremu Ose groups and did not observe any of the performers drank alcohol. Jaigbade specifically told me he did not drink alcohol. He also vouched, in a discussion with me, in June 2008, that his former rival and major Ilorin Dàdàkúàdá poet, the late Aremu Ose, never drank or allowed alcohol in his performance field. Yet, between 1985 and 1987 when I initially started the Dàdàkúàdá fieldwork and was always out at evenings observing their performances, I was not out to scrutinize them about what they drank, neither did I seek opportunity to confirm that what they sometime drank from cups was water or tea and not alcohol.

Another influence that the Muslim Ilorin has made on Dàdàkúàdá is on the drumming instruments. We cannot, however, refer to this as a direct Islamic influence. It is an influence made through the culture of some of the propagators of Islam to Ilorin (i.e. the Hausas). What Jaigbade has identified as a Hausa drum—*Akuba*—was introduced to Dàdàkúàdá performance in the twentieth century. Jaigbade claimed to be the first person to introduce *Akuba* to Dàdàkúàdá.[6] Yet, even though *Akuba* is now used by all Dàdàkúàdá performers, Dàdàkúàdá drumming patterns have not changed and neither has there any effort to imitate Huasa music or any such drumming like the *Bandiri* of the Muslim Quadiriyya performers. The case I discussed above of Waka songs in Dàdàkúàdá was a rarity.

Other areas of the Dàdàkúàdá artists' personal lives are influenced by the Islamic ethics in the community, and one of them is the dressing code. It is now common in Nigeria, Ilorin included, for people to adopt Hausa's *Babanriga* or *Agbada* (big gown) as evidence of Muslimness. The dresses of the Dàdàkúàdá artists are influenced by this tradition. Almost all the Dàdàkúàdá artists wear *Babanriga*, with a cap to match.[7] In fact, all the leading Dàdàkúàdá poets whom I have interviewed to date could not imagine a performance where they would wear shirts (which would have been a Western influence) or put on mere short-handed jumpers like *dasiki* (which would have been traditional Yoruba). Most of the artists I interviewed said they would wear jumper-like clothes only when there is lot of heat at the peak of performance as they would remove the big gown to have fresh air.[8] They insist that they would often go into any performance in big gowns.

Another very important impact of Islam on Dàdàkúàdá is the effect that strong opposition and condemnation by Ilorin *Alfas*[9] (Islamic scholars and preachers) have on Dàdàkúàdá artists. They condemn the poetry as highly un-Islamic and discourage people from patronizing the Dàdàkúàdá artists.[10] According to Jaigbade, this situation has forced the Dàdàkúàdá artists to work extra hard, "tirelessly hard" as Jaigbade described it, and to make their songs very interesting in such a way that *ee yan olee kati kuro n be man*[11]—"people cannot take their ears off it because of its sweetness to the ear; they cannot boycott us." It is also to counter this pressure from the Muslim preachers that the Dàdàkúàdá artists also learn the Quran and use Quranic verses in their songs. They want to show the community that they are also Muslims who read and know the Quran. They are eager to show that their songs can hold the esteem words and verses from the Quran.

However, this action of inserting Quranic verses in their songs on the part of the Dàdàkúàdá poets has only increased condemnation from the Ilorin Islamic scholars and preachers who see the inclusion of Quranic verses in non-Islamic songs as tantamount to a desecration or an abuse of the Quran. "How can one include words of God in the chants of the devil!" they seem to be querying, and they indeed consider Dàdàkúàdá as devilish songs or as poetry that can divert the Muslim fans from going to observe the daily Islamic salat (prayers) at its fixed times. Jaigbade, in my discussion of this issue with him, cited example of the Ilorin Islamic preachers who often attack Dàdàkúàdá to include Alfa Aminu, Alfa Agba, and Alfa Alabidun.[12]

It is no surprising that each side, the Muslim scholars and the Dàdàkúàdá artists, knows the other well. It is also certain that the Dàdàkúàdá artists have a lot to lose in Ilorin because of the strong sentiments the Ilorin people have always shown for Islam as a "native" religion just as they also show strong sentiment for Dàdàkúàdá as a "native" performance genre. Interestingly, there are now two meanings of nativity for Ilorin people: the claim of ownership they show for African traditions even as many of Ilorin people, because of Islam, are eager to disown the traditional African rituals and religious expressions in order to uphold Islamic tenants.

The second is the Ilorin indigenes' ownership of Islam as a new "worship of the soil" religion—*esin ilu*, indigenous religion. Even Yoruba oral traditional praise poetry (see *African Discourse in Islam, Oral Traditions, and Performance*) now acknowledges Ilorin as the Yoruba city that has discarded Yoruba Egungun cultic spirituality in forms of rejecting Egungun ancestral worship: *Ilu to bi to yi o leegun rara, esin leegin ile won, oko loro ibe* (see the Ilorin poem in Chapter 1). Ilorin is now the big Yoruba city without traces of Egungun masquerade! It is the city the Yoruba people now acknowledge in local folklore as "horses, its masquerades, swords are its custom"!

There is no wonder, therefore, that the Dàdàkúàdá artists work extra hard to ensure that they minimize any "damage" they might be assumed to be causing Islam or the new Muslim identity of Ilorin by the Ilorin Muslim scholars and preachers. They, however, show no apology that they too are Ilorin and are Muslims. Indeed, they are proud of being Ilorin and of being Dàdàkúàdá artists!

I have received many narratives that demonstrate this pride each time I spent time with Dàdàkúàdá artists, from Saka Kolobo to Olarewaju Oloje, and to Aremu Ose, Omoeke Amao, Odolaye Aremu, and Jaigbade Alao. In May 2008, Jaigbade narrated a story about how he influenced the choice of an Imam for the community mosque in his area of Ilorin. Two people were vying for the Imamship and one of them was quite desperate to take this position of spiritual headship of the mosque. They had to go to the then Emir of Ilorin, Sulukarnaini Gambari Mohammed, for adjudication. Sulukarnaini listened to all the elders who came with the delegation. He finally called on Jaigbade, who is an Oloye Oba, the traditional chief, to give him his insights. Jaigbade said he made it clear that the younger person who claimed to have more knowledge and energy should exercise patience as the elder person among the two contestants had more wisdom and better temperament to hold a community together. The Emir specifically commended Jaigbade for his wisdom, but said if Jaigbade had been asked to present his contributions in Dàdàkúàdá song, the entire audience would have found even more special sweetness in his presentation. Sulukarnaini asked the party to return to their community and ordered that the elder person be the new Imam. He told the younger one that he should continue to find more Islamic knowledge and that only God knew how such knowledge would help him tomorrow.

Jaigbade told me that when the Imam upheld by Sulukarnaini died, the younger person came to sought for his support and that he has given him such support.

It was certain that Jaigbade's story was intended for me to understand how influential he was in the mosque and among the people of his area even as he continued to be extremely influential in Dàdàkúàdá circles.

Notes

1 It is established that even the artists denounce anything that has to do with Egungun. They want to be seen as purely in the ways of Islam.
2 The homage to Allah is done here, in place of *Iba* which the Iwi chanters make to the ancestors.
3 Personal interview with Jimoh Jaigbade, 9 August 1987.
4 Ibid.
5 I did not come across anyone engaging in alcoholic drink in any of the performances I witnessed within Ilorin. This is not to saying that it is so outside Ilorin land. This is not also dismissing the possibility that few or all the artists consume beer, even in their houses!
6 Personal interview with Jimoh Jaigbade Alao, 9 August 1987.
7 This can be seen in the picture I included in this essay (see p. 69).
8 All the artists interviewed confirmed that.
9 *Alfas* means the Islamic mallams and preachers who are very versed in the Quran and the Hadith.
10 In fact, up till date, all Ilorin Islamic preachers condemn the nonreligious poets.
11 Personal interview with Jimoh Jaigbade Alao, 9 August 1987.
12 In fact, all Islamic preachers in Ilorin do, at one time or another, condemn the professional nonreligious poets. It was in 1984 that the popular annual *Were* competition called *Challengi* in which *Were* and later *Fuji* performers competed from night till dawn in Ilorin as part of the festival marking the end of the 30- or 29-day Ramadan fasting was criticized. The *Challengi* was later reformed by the then Emir of Ilorin, Alhaji Zulkarneini Gambari Mohammed, C.F.R. The Emir ordered that *Were* competition be dropped from the *Challengi* events for Quranic competition, and till date in Ilorin, Quranic reciters or chanters compete at the Emir's Palace on the eve of Eid al-Fitr.

5 Performance techniques

I have made attempts in the previous chapters to establish the place of performance in Dàdàkúàdá. This chapter, therefore, will take us through the various techniques used by the Dàdàkúàdá poets in presenting their art to the public and in informing and entertaining their fans. We may start by understanding how a person may think in the Yoruba community when he or she is presented with a singer or an oral artist. The Yoruba singer is called *Olorin*, owner of the song, or *Akorin*, the singer. Another word, *Alagbe*, which I have discussed earlier in this book citing my encounter with the late Omoeke Amao, is a more generic name and refers to both drummers and singers! *Agbe* is the name of the profession of singing or drumming! Specifically however, the drummer is called the *Onilu*, owner of the drum, or *Alulu*, the drummer. Each of these names, whichever one one chooses to use, indicates the relationship between an artist and the object of creativity, and that relationship is a realization, at least from the perspective of the Yoruba culture, of a performance act. The owner of a drum or the owner of a song is not the owner simply because he or she locks up the drum or the song in a box but because he or she performs them or uses them in his or her performance and lives his or her life from the dividends realized from such performance. He or she also serves society from the position of power of owning the drum or the song. In this sense, *akorin* (singer) or *alulu* (drummer) may serve only as secondary to the earlier names! It is this understanding, for example, that probably leads the Yoruba to describe the freelance drummer or singer as *alulu gbomi eko*, "the one who drums for water of porridge." The idea here is that the drummer or singer in question does not earn much and is only an itinerant singer or drummer (even a part-time singer or drummer in most cases). Yet, the meager amount that he or she earns has not in any way reduces his or her ownership of the drum or the song or the position of power which such ownership places on him or her. The nomadic singer, although committed, is not the big success-ful singer known from all areas of the community, he or she is only a small-scale singer, and earns a small-scale reward! But why is the performer, the oral artist in the Yoruba community in this profession and not in something else? Is it for the money or for the fame or for the cultural attachment to the tradition of singing and pre-serving society's history and protecting its culture? Is it, as Omoekee Amao said during my interview with him, that the Yoruba name for oral artist came from a phrase, *Ola gbee*, that is, "the wealthy, or the rich one has taken him or her away (to perform for them)" Or is he a performer to entertain and make his fan pleased, among others, as Oludare Olajubu suggested? One might ask, still, what is the function of the oral artist such as the Dàdàkúàdá artist, in society? This chapter will explore these and more questions with us. It will try to analyze the anatomy of Dàdàkúàdá-in-performance. Where is it performed? Who are the performers? What are the singing and the drumming tech-niques used? And the list is long.

Function of Dàdàkúàdá and places of its performance

Oludare Olajubu says that the aims of Yoruba oral artists are to please, to earn money, and to gain prestige.[1] This may be very much true of the African artists in general. Dàdàkúàdá artists are thus no exception.[2] In addition to this, however, the oral artists perform for personal joy and satisfaction. They personally derive pleasure in the act.[3] I have learned through my research into Dàdàkúàdá history that almost all the present and even the past Dàdàkúàdá poets came into the profession because of their personal interest in the art.[4] They had alternatives. They could have embarked on other full-term ventures that would have earned them a lot of money and prestige—especially since most of Muslim Ilorin look down on this kind of art.[5] Another important function of the Dàdàkúàdá artists is teaching people, es-pecially young people, their family lineage, and ancestral linings and genealogy.

Like other oral arts in Ilorin, Dàdàkúàdá is performed during wed-ding and naming ceremonies. Because of Islamic injunctions that en-courage Muslims to perform funeral rites quietly with only prayers and quiet mourning, no nonreligious songs or poetry like Dàdàkúàdá is employed during funeral rites in Ilorin. However, the Dàdàkúàdá singers are always invited from places like Kabba, Igbonna, and other Yoruba communities in the country to perform during funeral cere-monies. One can summarize, therefore, that Dàdàkúàdá functions as the art that enables people to celebrate their events and also help to promote cultural and community interactions. It also helps to transmit culture and oral history from generation to generation. Dàdàkúàdá oral art is performed outdoors in open fields. A partial circle is usually formed with the performing artists at an extreme end on every performance. Many members of the audience, most especially the uninvited guests, watch the performance standing. The invited guests are normally seated on chairs and benches. If a Dàdàkúàdá band must perform indoors, it has to be in a large hall that holds nothing less than 400 people. They also perform live on television and radio. Almost all the poets also make records, often now in cassette tapes, CDs, and DVDs, distributed throughout Nigeria.

Preparation for performances

There is no any special preparation to a Dàdàkúàdá field performance. The artists do not practice or rehearse before they go out to social occasions. They perform by improvisation. Mostly, the time of performance is the same time for the composition of the poems or one may put this the other way by saying that the Dàdàkúàdá artists perform the same time as they compose their songs. Odolaye Aremu explained to me that at the moment of performance, what they (artists) had never sung before come to their minds.[6] He said that if one was an *Oba* (a royal father) of a town who did the wishes of his people, the way the singers would praise him would reflect his true leadership activities: "God will put it on our mouth."[7]

However, it is important that scholars of African oral traditions do not overgeneralize whenever they discuss the issue of prior rehearsal by African oral performers. In Dàdàkúàdá in particular, there are rare occasions when Dàdàkúàdá artists rehearse. These are mostly when they are preparing to go to the recording studios for record, cassettes or DVDs. They try to arrange issues they want to sing about and ensure that every member artist in their group knows his part well, especially the *Boto*, the chorus group, and the head drummer. Jaigbade reaffirmed to me in a discussion in May 2008 that it was only when preparing for recording studio that he actually has a complete control of the actual songs his group sang. He said even before inviting his chorus group, he would have formulated every word and performance technique that would be used for the songs. As he has now acquired limited writing capability, he would even take papers and pen and get down all the dots and the commas he planned for the new record. Once he is ready with a complete performance, he would invite his group to a rehearsal or practice. He will direct them on exactly what to sing as a chorus and how to sing them.

It is not all the Dàdàkúàdá groups or artists that do this occasional rehearsal. Odolaye Aremu's group, for example, never rehearsed at all, even when going for record production! It was said that when one put Odolaye in a room and asked him to compose a song about a table, he would do it excellently.[8] This has also been said about the legendary Hausa poet, Shata Katsina (see Dandatti Abdul Kadir).

In preparation for field performance, each Dàdàkúàdá group gets its members together and moves collectively to the scene of performance. A field performance is truly an open performance and in an open venue! There is no prior practice whatsoever, and both the lead singer and the chorus exercise free performance judgment, showing extraordinary talents and performance expertise, improvising, and introducing new songs during performance. As they get to the performance venue, they set the modern-day microphone instrument and the loud speakers (amplifiers), placing them on the corners of the field. This is to enable their songs to be heard from near and far. Mostly, Dàdàkúàdá artists perform in the night, but they occasionally perform during the day. The night performances always last till dawn.[9] When an occasion calls for morning performance, the artists gladly embark on it.

Real performance

What is a real performance? It is that performance in which the Dàdàkúàdá group members are gathered together on the field of performance. This is not to say that a single Dàdàkúàdá artist cannot embark on a solo performance, or that such a solo performance would be an "unreal" performance. There are possibilities of individual freelance oral artists who combine singing with drumming and move around the community performing for their patrons. Nothing can be more real than that in a traditional African community! Such individual performers may also take moments to dance as they sing and beat their drums. The oral singers can be "all-rounders" and are happy to show off their skills. However, my definition of an actual "real Dàdàkúàdá performance," as the title above indicates, refers basically to a group performance, where every important member of a Dàdàkúàdá group in performance is present and the group is complete. In further discussion of the performance, we would have more to say about some important aspects or membership.

Leader

On the actual performance venue, the Dàdàkúàdá group divides into what can be described as subgroups. Each subgroup (the chorus subgroup, the drummers subgroup, the Boto subgroup, and the leader, lead singer, or head artist) stays on different sideways of their corner. The head artist who is also the leader normally stands in front of the chorus subgroup. Sometimes, he takes his place in the middle. His second-in-command (Omomose) stays close to him, to his right. This is the person who takes over when the head artist, or leader, takes a rest or when he has not surfaced for the day's performance. The leader normally is the main focus of the performance. He controls every artist under him. In Dàdàkúàdá, the entire group is called by the group leader's name, and the leader is basically the owner of the group! He is also a master leader in the sense that he is also teacher to all members of the chorus group who themselves plan to become a leader one day. Although the drummers subgroup has its own subleader who also occupies a major leadership position in the group and who earns the respect of other members as well of that of the fans, the drummer subleader must always defer to the overall group leader even in matters of choosing the drumming patterns desirable for a particular song. He is of course allowed to use his initiative as a professional drummer and often enjoys the final say in matter of drumming. In an interview with Jaigbade in May 2008, he reiterated the fact that as a singer and leader of the Dàdàkúàdá group, he is NOT an expert in matters of drumming; he said he is not a drummer and that matters of drumming is handled by the drummer. He almost shows emphasize in reiterating that the drummer is separately an expert, and he respects such expertise and does not take lightly the position of the drummer in a performance. However, it is clear to me when the Dàdàkúàdá group leader feels strongly opposed to any issue in his performance group, the leader's decision is final.

Chorus subgroup (Elegbe)

One may easily say that a Dàdàkúàdá performance is not complete without the participation of the Elegbe—the chorus subgroup. This can be easily called the chorus group; I call it a subgroup in the sense in which every Dàdàkúàdá group is one group, and each Dàdàkúàdá group is made up of subgroups. The chorus subgroup started in Dàdàkúàdá with an introduction of a solo *elegbe* (the solo chorus man) to the Dàdàkúàdá field performance.[10] The chorus subgroup is now made up of an *Omomose* (which was the name the initial solo man was called) and six or seven other subgroup members. In some occasions, there is a five-member subgroup.[11] The *Omomose* (the pupil knows his art well!), as the leader of the subgroup and assistant of the Dàdàkúàdá group leader, takes the lead in chorusing. This is because he is often the most senior member of the chorus subgroup, sometimes the most knowledgeable of the group activities. He knows the appropriate chorus line after every verse chanted by the leader. When I said before that the chorus group exercises judgment and spontaneous improvisation and may introduce new songs during performance, and separate from the songs been sung by the group leader, it is the subgroup leader that provides such leadership to the chorus group, and the members of the chorus group always follow his cue. In fact, it is him, the Omomose, that makes such a call, and his subgroup members all follow his lead! Jaigbade Alao said that the creation of the chorus subgroup was to allow a resting time for the group leader.[12] When the chorus subgroup members are chorusing, the group leader rests and thinks over the next song to chant. Yet as has been said, apart from a verse repeated after the leader or dictated by him, the chorus subgroup (through Omomose) initiates appropriate chorus songs to different songs by the lead artist.

The drummers subgroup (Onilu)

This subgroup is made up of the head drummer and other drummers who drum following the cues from the head drummer. There is no determination about how many drummers can be in a Dàdàkúàdá group. There could be a few set of drummers that use the same drums, but most drummers beat different type or shape of drums in accompanying the Dàdàkúàdá performance. The agogo (gong) and sekere bearers are also part of the drummers subgroup. This subgroup is responsible for accompanying the songs with danceable drummings. They are highly respected by the Dàdàkúàdá lead singer and all members of the Elegbe. The head drummer is especially accorded a lot of honor. I will discuss the Dàdàkúàdá drummers again soon in this chapter.

Boto

The *Boto* is the Chief messenger to the Dàdàkúàdá-group-in-performance. He conveys the message from members of the audience to the lead artist. He passes requests for special verses or praise songs for special people to the lead artist. *Boto* stops the play and delivers the message or requests of a fan. His name, *Boto* (*bo ba to*), is a subordinate clause of a longer statement. The longer statement is: *Bo ba to (baa ba lo to) Onilu asi sinmin, aikoto onilu a kan abuku*—"When (we say) it's enough, the drummer would have to stop drumming, otherwise the drummer would be rebuked."

Many people have abbreviated this statement to *Boto*, which really on its own may have no apparent meaning. The *Boto* also announces and carries gifts from the fans to the lead artist or any member of the performing group. During performance, he occasionally reminds the leader of important names and even family lineages. He also makes jests and passes jokes loudly. He is rightly described as "an announcer, an interpreter and a human loudspeaker."[13] He uses lots of humor on the stage and makes the field performance really fun for the fans. Some *Boto* become very popular in the community, and oftentimes, the lead artist makes references to them in his songs during performance. Some *Boto* serve as the lead artist's good memory, reminding him issues he might have not remember during performance but which would instantly be of interest to the fans. In most cases, the lead artist is grateful to a brilliant and sharp-minded *Boto*. I was told of instances in the history of Dàdàkúàdá when a *Boto* was more popular than the lead drummer (subleader) and where fans come to see a Dàdàkúàdá performance because of the attraction of the *Boto*. In most cases, the fans know and can name *Boto* of different Dàdàkúàdá groups in the community by heart.

Introduction (the beginning of performance)

The beginning of Dàdàkúàdá performance, which is often the introductory stage, has changed from the recitation of just a line at the inception of the development of Dàdàkúàdá, "Da-da-dada kua da," to a payment of homage and a making of opening prayer often in the Islamic ways. In the following example, the Dàdàkúàdá group declares that it begins in the name of Allah. The group offers prayers for progress and success as well:

LEADER: Bisi mi llahi al-Rahamani Rahimi
CHORUS: Bisi mi llahi al-Rahamani Rahimi
LEADER: Makaana aliyya
CHORUS: Makaana aliyya
LEADER: Warafa'a na u
CHORUS: Makaana aliyya[14]

LEADER: In the name of Allah, the Beneficient, the Merciful
CHORUS: In the name of Allah, the Beneficient, the Merciful
LEADER: In high position
CHORUS: In high position
LEADER: We (Allah) exalted him
CHORUS: In high position

It can be seen that the artist's prayer is recited in Arabic. They are taken directly from the verses of the Holy Quran. This is one of the important aspects of Dàdàkúàdá today, and the artist is always eager to show case his Islamicity. It may also be said that the offering of a prayer in Arabic and especially from the Quran is an evidence of the Dàdàkúàdá group's current reality and social habit rather than any efforts to satisfy the hugely Islamic community. This is true in light of the manners in which a typical Ilorin person has adopted the Islamic modes into the cultural patterns of his or her daily performance of life. Such communion forms like *salamu alaikum* (greetings), *aleykumu salamu* (response), *alhamdulillahi* (expression of satisfaction), and even *barika* (greetings, which is taken from the Hausa language, which initially had taken it from Arabic) are all evidences of the deep-rooted Muslim expressive cultures in Ilorin. It must also be said that the Dàdàkúàdá group may offer opening songs in entirely Ilorin Yoruba language and not use an Arabic language or Quranic verse whatsoever.

The performance body (or the middle of performance)

The songs chanted are mostly praise songs (*Oriki*). It is at this stage that people come to offer money or other gifts to the artists in appreciation of his praises for them or perhaps to show gratitude to the ways he has composed and delivered his songs. Among other forms of gifts also offered to a Dàdàkúàdá artist are usually goats, cows, cloths, and ornament, and there have been reports of when a patron gave the hand of his daughter in marriage to a Dàdàkúàdá singer, although really rare in the late twentieth- and the twenty-first-century Ilorin city. Also when people make requests for who should be praised, such requests are made with gifts for the lead artist through the *Boto*. Of all the Dàdàkúàdá performance songs, *Oriki*—praise songs—alone can be said to take more than 70%. The remaining percentage covers the messages of the artists on moral, social, cultural, and political matters. This is not to say that the praise songs do not contain messages on all these areas.

The middle stage, or the body of performance, is also the place where the artists display various artistic skills and performance techniques. These skills are evident in their use of language, dancing, gesticulating, and other movements of the body. The normal dancing pattern of the Dàdàkúàdá artists-in-performance is not as active or vigorous as that of their fans. Mostly, the Dàdàkúàdá artists just make minor movements of parts of their bodies. It is the *Boto* that often exercises more freedom to dance more actively on the performance field.

Generally, the performance techniques traditional to Dàdàkúàdá are five, and they include the simultaneous delivery technique, the talking-level technique, the dialogue technique, the lead-and-follow technique, and the take-a-break technique. The following are examples of the performances in each of the above-named Dàdàkúàdá performance techniques:

a) The simultaneous delivery technique

Before we examine an example of this type of performance technique, it is important to state here that it was mostly Odolaye Aremu who used this technique as a dominant technique in his performance during his lifetime. Performers, who have continued in Odolaye's tradition, including Odolaye's former chorus group, have continued to perform and to use this technique.[15] This technique was the basic performance technique during the initial stage of Dàdàkúàdá's development when only two or three artists, including the drummer, were involved in every performance.[16] The leader and one member (named Omomase) accompanying singer normally sang simultaneously. Actually, in this technique, the leader initiates songs; the accompanying artist tries to imitate the leader by chanting simultaneously with the leader, tracing the leader's voice. This accompanying artist is the same that is also sometimes called *elegbe* by the Yoruba.[17] In performing this technique in contemporary Dàdàkúàdá, the leader and all the Elegbe members sing simultaneously.

Example (Odolaye and Elegbe—chorus group):

Eni yan soro eman se f'eniyan sere
Nje baa reke o a se be ni re ni (pause)
A a ye e,
Eru aaye yi le bami pupo ojo

Omo eyan ti gbegi togun laase
Aye n binu n kanhun, won da kahun somi
Aye n binu iyo, won dayo s'eepe
Aye n binu Edu, nni won ba geka Edu ku
Kan.[18]

People are difficult, please never take people lightly
When we see a cunning person, we might think he is a good person.
A a yee! This world!

I'm afraid of this world indeed,
The child of man who cuts the tall tree underneath,
When the world is annoyed of *Kanhun* (potassium) they pour
    Kanhan into water.
When the world is angry with *Iyo* (salt) they pour *Iyo* on the sand.
When the world is angry with Edu, they cut all Edu's fingers
    but one!

When Odolaye is performing this particular song, we can hear the trailing or simultaneous voices that sing it with him. It is interesting that Odolaye maintained this tradition into the late twentieth century when he died, and that some others have actually carried the tradition after him into the twenty-first century. Every Dàdàkúàdá group may use this technique from time to time during performance. Yet, those who still use it as a dominant performing tradition are very few in Dàdàkúàdá.

b) The talking-level technique
    As the name of this performance technique implies, the song is performed on the normal talking level. This technique has never dominated the Dàdàkúàdá performance at any state of the genre's development. It is occasionally used in the performance to explain one or two things or to elaborate on an issue. Interestingly, even though all Dàdàkúàdá artists use this technique, Odolaye Aremu used it more than any other Dàdàkúàdá poets. Let us consider the following example from his group.
    Example (Odolaye and Elegbe):

Bo ba lo laya, Olowo lowo, oo
Man ra mato, oo maa gbe lo Sokoto,
Oo maa gbe lo Safara, awon aye, won
Le maje o lo bi kankan.[19]

If you claim to be brave, and to be rich,
to start buying vehicles, and start journeying to Sokoto,
and journeying to Safara, the world,
they may make you go nowhere.

It is used sometimes to quickly highlight some issues, and oftentimes, especially by Dàdàkúàdá poets other than Odolaye, they are in the form of phrases and short sentence. Odolaye often went several songs above that as can be seen in the example above.

c) The dialogue technique

The dialogue technique is popular with the audience and used by all the Dàdàkúàdá artists. It ceased, however, to be the main feature of performance as it used to be during the third stage of Dàdàkúàdá's development.[20] Here, there is a kind of dialogue between the leader and *Omomose* or *elegbe*, the chorus group.

Example:

AJIBAYE: Omomose

OMOMOSE: Eegun alare,
            Se ko si nkan kan?

AJIBAYE: Ntodaa ni m bee

OMOMOSE: Nkan be ni ko si nkan kan,
            Eegun alare Baba Olokooba, Jandulku Baba Raimi

AJIBADO: Nso nle Oba
            Ni le bale mi, oko mi
            Sulu omo Oba,
            Gambari oko Sefi Igbaja,
            Gambari omo Laofe ni Ilorin.
            Sulu baalee mi,
            Gambari baalee mi o.

OMOMOSE: Sulu baalee mi,
            Gambari baalee mi o.

AJIBAYE: Sulu baalee mi,
            Gambari baalee mi o.

OMOMOSE: Sulu baalee mi o.
            Gambari baalee mi o.[21]

AJIBAYE: Omomose

OMOMOSE: Eegun alare,
            I hope there's no problem

AJIBAYE: There is a good tiding

OMOMOSE: So, there is nothing but something
            Eegun alare, father of Olokooba,
            Janduku, father of Raimi.

AJIBAYE: Proceed to the Emir's palace
            In the house of my master, my husband,

Sulu, the Prince,
Gambari, the husband of Sefi Igbaja,
Gambari, the offspring of Laofe in Ilorin
Sulu, my master,
Gambari, my master o

OMOMOSE: Sulu, my master,
Gambari, my master o.
AJIBAYE: Sulu, my master,
Gambari, my master o.
OMOMOSE: Sulu, my master,
Gambari, my master o.

Perhaps one of the reasons why the audience likes this technique is that it enables them to join the Omomose in responding to the lead artist whenever they have mastered the songs or especially when a popular song that they have memorized is being performed, and it gives them the sense of entering into a dialogue with the lead artist during a field performance.

d) The lead-and-follow technique
This technique is very similar to "the call and response" style in *Iwi* performance as identified by Olajubu.[22] The difference is that in Dàdàkúàdá, both the chorus and the drummers wait for the leader (or head singer) to lead before they follow. There is, therefore, a clear time space between the lead artist's song and the chorus's following or responding. That is why the role of each of them (chorus, drummers, and the leader) is always distinct. There is no situation in this performance technique in which the lead artist, the chorus, and the drumming group perform simultaneously. The leader is usually allowed to come first.[23] We will consider an example from Jaigbade Alao's group.
Example:

LEAD (JAIGBADE): Kole-ba wa logigi ma o
Kole bawa logigi ma o
Aroye nise wa, kee su wa,
Kole ba wa logigi ma o.

FOLLOW (CHORUS): Kole ba wa logigi ma o
Kole ba wa logigi ma o
Aroye nise wa, kee su wa,
Kole ba wa logigi ma oo.

LEAD (JAIGBADE):	Ko ti e gbodo bawa logigi, Orin ni see ti wa, Aa kuku sise mii kun, Orin nise wa. Ojo ohun mo ro ree mi, Salmanu Ajani Maloko oko Iya Kudi, Ajani Maloko omo Anasara, Ore mi Ajani Omo Jimoh, Omo Eko tin fun wa lowo nlanla
FOLLOW (CHORUS):	Kole ba wa logigi ma o, Kole ba wa logigi ma o Aroye ni se wa, kee su wa, Kole bawa logigi ma oo.[24]
LEAD:	It cannot take us by surprise It can't take us by surprise Rhetoric is our art, it never tires us It cannot take us by surprise again
FOLLOW:	It cannot take us by surprise It can't take us by surprise Rhetoric is our art, it never tires us It cannot take us by surprise again.

LEAD:	It can never take us unprepared,
	Singing is our art,
	We have no other work,
	Singing is our work.
	It's that day I saw my friend,
	Salmanu Ajani Maloko, the husband of
	    Iya Kudi;
	Ajani Maloko, the offspring of Anasara,
	My friend Ajani, offspring of Jimoh,
	the child of Lagos, who gives us money in
	    plenty.

FOLLOW:	It cannot take us by surprise, It cannot take us by surprise Rhetoric is our art, it never tires us It cannot take us by surprise again.

e) The take-a-break technique

The take-a-break technique is usually introduced when Dàdàkúàdá performance reaches a climax at the performing field. It is otherwise called *O too edure na*. Here, the leader asks the subgroups to stop for a while. This, most especially, affects the drummers group—drumming is also stopped. The lead artist then chants his lengthy poem for some time, while the chorus subgroup repeats each one after him. The drums remain silent. The lead singer ends the lengthy chanting with a kind of lyric song. The chorus as usual takes up this ending chorus song and the drummers then came in beating their drums simultaneously. A series of the technique is performed progressively. Again, let us consider some of this performance from Jaigbade's group.

Example:

JAIGBADE: O to, edurona

CHORUS: O to, edurona

JAIGBADE: Je n la, je n lowo o
Je n la, je n lowo

CHORUS: Je n la, je n lowo o
Je n la, je n lowo

JAIGBADE: Je n la, je n lowo o
Je n la, je n lowo

CHORUS: Je n la, je n lowo
Je n la, je n lowo

JAIGBADE: M'be lohun oba,
Je n la je n lowo lowo

CHORUS: Olohun Oba je nla je n lowo lowo.

JAIGBADE: O to, eduro na

CHORUS: O to, eduro na

JAIGBADE: Ayinla Olowo

CHORUS: Ayinla Olowo

JAIGBADE: Elepo Aran, ewole erora

CHORUS: Elepo Aran, ewole erora

JAIGBADE: Saka Eleduku, ewole erora

CHORUS: Saka Eleduku, e wole erora

JAIGBADE: E maa rora, Akanho omo Ogbondoko ni ile Ajibaye

CHORUS: E maa rora, Akanho omo Ogbondoko ni ile Ajibaye

JAIGBADE: Saarumii,
            Ajibaye e
            Ogbondokooo
            Saaruumi o

CHORUS: Saarumi i,
            Ajibaye e
            Ogbodoko o o
            Saaruumi O.[25]

JAIGBADE: It's enough, wait a while

CHORUS: It's enough, wait a while

JAIGBADE: May I prosper, may I be rich (with money)

CHORUS: May I prosper, may I be rich (two times)

JAIGBADE: I'm praying to God Almighty,
            May I prosper, may I be rich

CHORUS: God Almighty, may I prosper, may I be rich

JAIGBADE: It's enough, wait a while

CHORUS: It's enough, wait a while

JAIGBADE: Ayinla Olowo

CHORUS: Ayinla Olowo

JAIGBADE: Elepo Aran, you're welcome

CHORUS: Elepo Aran, you're welcome

JAIGBADE: You're welcome, Akanho, offspring of Ogbondoko
            in the compound of Ajibaye

CHORUS: You're welcome, Akanho, offspring of Ogbondoko
            in the compound of Ajibaye

JAIGBADE: Saarumii,
            Ajibaye e
            Ogbodokooo
            Saaruumi o

CHORUS: Saarumii,
            Ajibaye e
            Ogbodokooo
            Saaruumi o

Conclusion (the ending or idagbere—*farewell)*

At the end of every performance, the artists sing *Orin Idagbere*, farewell songs. It is a way of informing the teaming audience that the performance has come to the end, and that the artists are grateful of the audience's love and support, but that the artists must end the performance and leave now, and the audience and the patrons should also be prepared to accept the artists' decision. It is not surprising that the artists feel the responsibility to properly end their performance by singing the *idagbere* song, because there seems to be a strong bond between the artists and the audience, and it is not uncommon that the audience may want the performance to continue when the artists feel the opposite. The word *idagbere*, means saying the "good bye, we will meet again," as is evident in the songs performed by the artists at this juncture.

Example:

LEADER: A n rele o

CHORUS: Layo layo la o fi pade

LEADER: Afe maa lo

CHORUS: Layo layo la o fi pade

LEADER: Ani koolohun so pade kowa

CHORUS: Babaloke, soo pade kowa.[26]

LEADER: We're going home o

CHORUS: We shall meet in happiness

LEADER: We want to go

CHORUS: We shall meet in happiness

LEADER: May God ensure that we meet (in happiness)

CHORUS: May God ensure that we meet (in happiness)

LEADER: Father-above, ensure we meet (in happiness)

CHORUS: May God ensure we meet (in happiness).

As this song is performed, it is common to see the members of the audience begin to disperse, and the drummers begin to drum in tones that indicate that drumming is also about to come to the end. The whole performance field enters into a new dispersal mood, and suddenly the drum, the chorus subgroup, and the lead artist come to a stop!

The drum language in Dàdàkúàdá

Gangan is the major drum used in Dàdàkúàdá. Generally speaking, the Dàdàkúàdá drumming implements include *Akuba, Emele, Iyaalu, Agogo, Aropo, Pakeke,* and *Kongoro.* There are two main patterns of drum beatings, patterns or rhythms (whichever one it is called will be correct) in Dàdàkúàdá. They are the *Pami oduku* or *Ogere* and *Woro* patterns. The *Pami oduku* rhythm is the faster of them. It is used when the performance is at its climax. Also, it is usually the drumming pattern used when women are dancing. This is because women dance very actively and very quickly, twisting their hips and buttocks. This drumming pattern is also referred to as *Ilu alujo,* the drum pattern for dancing. In fact, the songs to this pattern are called *Ogere.* The second drumming pattern is *Woro,* the same name that songs to it bear. This pattern is used when the performance is slow—the dance to it is usually done very gently, slowly, and majestically. Oftentimes, the men do this dancing, but it could also be the women dancing. The majority of Dàdàkúàdá artists use the two patterns at variance. Again, an exception to this is Odolaye Aremu, who uses the *Pami-Oduku* predominantly. Odolaye's singing and drumming are usually very fast.

The Dàdàkúàdá head drummer (who I have referred to as the drummers subgroup leader) beats the *Iyaalu,* a kind of big *gangan* drum regarded as the mother of all the drums. He controls the other drummers and, in accordance with the songs of the artists, introduces the fitting-drumming pattern that other drummers follow. His position is very important in the Dàdàkúàdá group. As I already discussed, he exercises a great deal of power. He has autonomy to some degree. This is largely because the lead singer is usually unskilled in drumming and may not often concern himself with it. The lead singer relies heavily on the head drummer.[27] The head drummer often uses his *gangan* drum to remind the lead artist some important things, including family lineages. He thus also serves (like the *Boto*) as a memory of the lead singer. He also drums many proverbs and adages. The *gangan* drum is indeed the talking drum! The members of the audience who often have ears for the drums and carefully listen to the drums as they follow the songs. Often, the audience sings along with the drum when they drum proverbs or any popular adage. For example, the lead artist may be singing about the coming year and what he expects of the community next year, and suddenly the drummer may introduce this songs through his drum: *Ododun la nrorogbo, ododun lan rawusa, ododun lan rooma obi ninu ate!* "Every year we see the *orogbo* nut, every year we see the *awusa* nut, every year we see the coconut pieces in the market!"

The lead singer, having heard the drummer's song or proverb, may or may not sing along with him. However, it is actually usual for the lead singer to direct his next song to thank the drummer and also sings after the drummer. The lead artist may respond thus: *Mo gbo ntowi onilu mi.* "I heard what you said my drummer"! The head drummer also constantly beats in proverbs that are relevant to the songs being performed by the lead artist. For example, when the lead artist is singing about a person who just completed a task, and congratulating him or her for a job well done, the head drummer may drum the following: *Nibi ise eni laati moni lole, Salawu ku ise!* "It is at one's work that one may know if a person is lazy, Salawu, well done"! Or commending an achievement or an award, the drummer could drum *Asense tun se to ba sayi tan o semi si o, asen se tun se!* "You'll accomplish more, after this one, you'll achieve even more"! When an important patron enters into the performance field and the lead artist has not noticed, the drummer may drum this as a clue to the leader: *otide, otide, omo oko, otide, omo agbaje otide, omo sarumi, otide, ogbondoko, otide!* "He's here, he's here, true son of his father, he's here, the child of Agbaje, he's here, the child of Sarumi, he's here, Ogbondoko, he's here"! The lead artist may then thank the drummer through his songs and immediately begin to welcome the important patron to the field. He may begin to sing new songs and invite the chorus subgroup to introduce new chorus about the patron as well. When it is time to go and the lead singer continues to sing, the drummer may remind the lead singer, it is time we sing the orin idagbere, the bye-bye song. The drummer may begin to drum: *ajo kole dun dun kama rele, ile ni ibusimi oko!* "We cannot enjoy a trip so much as to not return to our homes. The home is where one returns to rest"! There is nothing the Iyaalu drummer cannot say through his drum. The talking drum phenomenon is more than what most people who are not exposed to it might understand. It is a whole different tradition on its own and enormously popular and often independent of the oral singer, even when some singers are themselves drummers!

Audience participation

The audience's major role in the real performance is to clap or applaud the artists or even sing along with the oral artists. They also show appreciation to the artists by offering generous gifts to them. Generally speaking, however, the judgment of the audience on every artists goes a long way to contribute to the popularity or otherwise of any Dàdàkúàdá poet. There is, however, no formalized way of registering such a judgment other than to respond to the artists performance spontaneously on the field of performance, either through offering gifts to them or by clapping for them or getting to the dancing floor. It is also the member of the audience who carries the news of the artists' expertise and skills to all the nooks and corners of the community and thus spreads the news about the new talents and unique poets that no one else can beat in the art!

Also, the celebrant(s) who invited the professional Dàdàkúàdá artists to perform for them and their guests may dance on the field of the performance while also showing approval for the performance. Those who appreciate the songs "spray" the artists with money or sometimes they offer the artist money to show solidarity with the celebrant. It is often the case among the Yoruba that the community notices when guests show solidarity with the celebrants, which is seen as giving the celebrant an *Iyi* and *Eye*! Some send their donations to the lead artist through *Boto*. Many also give out cows, clothes, and other valuable materials to the Dàdàkúàdá artists, including bicycles, motorcycles, and cars.[28]

Apprenticeship in Dàdàkúàdá

A person who wants to become a Dàdàkúàdá poet may undergo training under any of the many Dàdàkúàdá lead artists in Ilorin land. The first requirement to apprenticeship is that one must have a good voice that the lead artist feels satisfied with.[29] Also, an *Alaafa* or Islamic Mallam may be consulted to find out whether, in the words of a Dàdàkúàdá lead artist, "eje re ba ti wa mu"[30] ("his blood suits ours"). That is to say whether an apprentice's admission to the group will bring chaos and destruction or peace and progress for the other members.

An apprentice is expected to follow the lead artist everywhere the latter goes to perform. He also comes to his house frequently and stays sometimes with the leader during the day. This is because an apprentice is not only expected to learn the skill of performance on the Dàdàkúàdá field but also to acquire the ideas and philosophies of the lead artists.[31] Usually, there is no agreement to the number of years an apprentice will spend as everything depends on his acquiring the skills, his intelligence, and expertise.

A fresh apprentice starts by staying with the chorus subgroup. He observes their activities and later joins in chorusing. An apprentice gradually gets promoted and may rise to the position of head of the chorus subgroup. He reaches the zenith of his training when he becomes the second-in-command (Omomose) to the lead artist and stands by the right side of the lead artist during a performance.[32]

There is no ceremony or rite to the departure or graduation of an apprentice. Some apprentices do break away without the consent of the leader. Oftentimes, this action may lead to serious conflict with the leader as he is not happy at the sudden departure, and may even feel betrayed. It is even possible for such action on the part of the apprentice to cause enmity with his master. However, it is also possible for the two people to eventually resolve this conflict when the former eventually apologizes even though he remains independent and now a leader of his own group. Some who acquire the leaders' consent are usually given some drumming implements and are prayed for by the leader. An apprentice normally spends as much as six, seven, eight, or even nine years in training. The duration of apprenticeship can be less or more depending on the circumstances.[33]

Notes

1 I.O. Olajubu, "Iwi Egungun chants in Yoruba Oral Literature," M.A. Thesis, U of Lagos (1970): 60–61.
2 Omoeke Amao and other artists interviewed express this view.
3 This is the first reason all the artists I interviewed gave for their decision to be Dàdàkúàdá poets. They say, in fact, that the satisfaction they derive in performing is more than what the listeners derive.
4 Jaigbade Alao, most especially, says that he left his former art, *Agbe*, for Dàdàkúàdá because he was enticed by the poetry of Ajigbaye, a former Dàdàkúàdá poet.
5 They regard the poetry as un-Islamic.
6 Personal interview with Odalaye Aremu, 12 August 1987.
7 Ibid.
8 Personal interview with Bayo Alayande, 3 September 1987.
9 I attended several night performances for recording on tape for this project. I normally stay in the performances from around ten in the night to the dawn of the following day.
10 This was the composition at the first stage of Dàdàkúàdá's development. Explanations on this are in Chapter 3.
11 This exempts Odolaye's group. He usually has one *elegbe* who sings simultaneously with him.
12 Personal interview with Jaigbade Alao, 9 August 1987.
13 Y.A. Ajayi, "Asa: A Public Entertainment in Ilorin Area, Kwara State," M.A. Thesis, Department of Linguistics and Nigerian Languages, U of Ibadan (1982): 43–44.
14 Personal interview with Jaigbade Alao, 9 August 1987. He also recites this at his performance I recorded on 30 December 1987.
15 This can be heard in all his records and field performances.
16 This has been thoroughly explained in another chapter.
17 Though other Dàdàkúàdá poets have an *elegbe* who sings simultaneously with the head artist (same as lead artist or group leader), they maintain a separate subgroup for chorusing purposes. Odolaye has no such group.
18 Odolaye Aremu, "E Saalo Faye," Olatunbosun Records ORCNP 151A, 1982.

19 Ibid.
20 Explanations are in Chapter 3.
21 Jaigbade chants these lines for me during one of my interviews with him, 9 August 1987.
22 I.O. Olajubu, "Iwi Egungun Chants in Yoruba Oral Literature," M.A. Thesis, U of Ibadan (1970): 101.
23 All the Dàdàkúàdá artists I interviewed always emphasized this as a mark difference between Dàdàkúàdá and other Yoruba songs and poetry in performance.
24 Jaigbade Alao, "Kole ba wa logigi," Chief Records LPCRL 001 B, 1987.
25 An excerpt from the performance of Jaigbade Alao recorded on 30 December 1987 in Ile Igbonna, Edun, Ilorin.
26 Ibid; Jaigbade Alao also chanted this during an interview on 9 August 1987.
27 Personal interview with Bayo Alayande, 3 September 1987.
28 Jaigbade Alao was given a 504 Station Wagon car by one Adisa Alamanyo, was given a Jeep vehicle (*jiipu*) by the Olofa of Offa Oba Mufutua Gbadamasi and a bus by the Zanna of Ilorin, Engineer Lanre Sagaya. Omoeke Amao had also been given a Volvo car in the past.
29 Personal interview with Omoeke Amao, 8 August 1987.
30 Ibid.
31 Ibid.
32 Ibid.
33 Omoeke Amao was an apprentice under Jaigbade Alao for nine years.

6   Politics, partisanship, and traditional oral poetry
An example of Odolaye Aremu

Traditional African oral poets are very much involved in the politics of their societies. Apart from the specialized oral singers like the palace poets who are constantly in palaces and singing for and about community leaders, most other African oral singers have similar license to sing about sociopolitical situations of their people. Indeed, the formalist's ideology of an art-for-art sake is alien to many African communities, certainly to the Yoruba community of Nigeria. Politics, in view of the Yoruba, seems not to be limited to party politics and election politics, as people appear to practice in the Western world. The Yoruba politics includes politics at home, at workplace, and at the larger society. For example, the husband's dealings with his wife at home is regarded as political, and how he is able to treat the home situation determines how much he is respected as a good politician in the community. Also, the wife's dealing with her husband, and in polygamy, wives' dealings among themselves, is politics.

There is politics in the extended family system, at the marketplace, among the farmers, the hunters, the goldsmiths, the religious priests, in fact, at the village or town administration levels as a whole. This is why the concept of politics among the Yoruba is different from what the white colonizers brought forward to Africa and does still not agree with the postcolonial narrow view of who is a politician and who is not, as is the case in the Western-style political setups in Africa.

Politics, among the traditional Yoruba, it seems to me, is more of community administration and community responsibility. It is an art where tradition, experience, and proficiency come to play. For example, when an *alaafin*, King of Oyo, wants to take a decision, he considers the political and social implications of such a decision on his people. He involves the "Oyo Mesi" members of the traditional ruling council and sometimes even allows a discussion among professional groups such as farmers groups, hunters group, bricklayers group, or even throw the issue for an open discussion at the community square involving all interested community members. Our definition of politics here is what Yoruba calls "abasepo," "asepo," or "oselu," that is, interpersonal relationship, community administration. It includes all kinds of relationships, between the young and the old, men and women, the king and his people, the marketers and their customers. Everybody is important in this relationship and must be allowed to play his or her role. An *alaafin* that would not involve the *Oyo Mesi* and the community in discussions is most often not considered a good leader. An elder, a husband, or a mother that would not seek for opinion in administering the home, is not a good politician either. Dialogue, which may be translated into Yoruba as *àsàrò,* is at the heart of the concept of politics among the Yoruba. The Yoruba have an adage, *Omode gbon, agba gbon lafi da ile Ife,* "the wisdom of both a child and the elder combine to found the Ife town." Ife is regarded as the cradle of the Yoruba. There are Yoruba oral traditions that explain how the Yorubas descended from Ife. The importance of a participatory politics in the Yoruba culture cannot be more strongly expressed than has been done in the above Yoruba proverb.

Why am I starting my discussion of partisanship in Yoruba oral poetry with this? It is perhaps to show that however politically partisan the African oral poet decides to get, he or she is only being true to the traditional political culture of his or her community. The Yoruba oral poets play very significant roles in the politics of their communities. My intention in this chapter is to use mainly examples of Odolaye Aremu and slightly of a few others as well, excerpts from their songs and political activities from the 1960s to early 1990s, to show that despite contemporary influences from Euro-American cultures on Nigeria, the traditional Yoruba poets never abandoned their traditional roles in politics.

Yoruba songs and politics: the home, the village, and the palace

Perhaps, the home is the most important place where the Yoruba utilize poetry to express political thoughts. Poetry is explored as a satire at home to correct what is considered "bad policies" and to encourage good interaction among members of the family. For example, one of the first songs a child may grow up to know is the traditional lineage poetry of his family. This is called the "Oriki orile" or "oriki irumole" lineage poetry. This is the poetry in different versions that his or her immediate parents and extended family elders chant for the child as they acknowledge courtesies from the child and as they respond to his or her traditional salutations at different times of the day. Freelance poets are also on hand to perform the child's lineage poetry as they praise his or her parents and relatives, all to the child's hearing and seeing. In this poetry, the various stories about his/her foreparents are narrated. These include the foreparent's relationship with his people at home and abroad, the honors they brought to the family, their senses of justice, and other characteristics they were known for during their lifetimes. They include the history of how the family or the community was founded and sometimes even of the gods and goddesses worshipped in the household or the community as a whole. Such poetry does not shy away from whatever is considered "negative" actions of the foreparents. It is expected that every child will learn from the songs and formulate his or her own political and social philosophies from them. The following praise poetry (see Ogunjimi and Na'Allah 2005: 60)[1] is from Soke family in Owu, Abeokuta, one of the five ruling houses in Owuland:

O see, pele oko mi
Iloko omo Arelu
Omo otileta biisu
Eru masa, omo ajoba lele
Tetu won joba lohun ero
Omo pana jare ana
O pana tan o tun tii mo'le
Amu'da mimu fi be ana lori
Won d'eni ba se ni loore laa lu pa
Omo aketa l'ona osi eta
Sewe sewe Iloko, ema mo se sigo
Eni to se sigo lo da'le
Eni to se sigo l'eke
Otun iloko ti mu ida odele
Osi iloko ti mu ida odero
Arin gbungbun loko ti mu da
O di beri
Ko seni to je le e lenu
Kabiyesi oo

...Thanks, my dear one
Ikolo, the child of Arelu
The descendant of he who springs up like a yam tuber
from the soil

Eru masa, the child of He who becomes king by force
They must be king at all cost
He who kills his in-law and justifies it
He kills his in-law and imprisons him
He who uses a sharp sword to behead his in-law
They say it is he that helps them that they must kill
The descendants of Aketa along the road of Osieta
Iloko, do not attend sigo
He who attends Sigo is a traitor
He who attends Sigo is a liar
Iloko, hi right hand employs sword to fight
Iloko, his left hand employs sword for peace
Iloko walks, sword-in-hand to behead
No one dares querry you
Kabiyesi!

An elderly woman performed the above lineage poetry to praise a young child. We can easily trace the genealogical tree of the child through the poetry. We also know that he is a descendant of a very brave and courageous ruling family. His great-grandfather—the king—detested cheating and beheaded even his in-law when they cheated, as he considered justice demanded. But we also know that his descendants take kingship by force. His family members are warriors. Except we try to understand their sociocultural background we may not be able to judge their actions. The poetry affords the child to know the value of his family and the entire community and to decide on the line of his own greatness in life.

Our next example is from "Orin owe," "proverbial" or satirical songs usually sung among housewives often in a polygamous family. In this case, the husband is a very responsible husband. His wife thus sings his praises and tells the community that he is worthy of emulation. The song is rendered in Moba dialect of Ondo:

Emi lomo eleregun kege ni jeji oye
Eleregun kege nii je Edemo lule mi
Mibolomo ulo
Me boluya eniyan ire
Oni mo jijo irugbo ose
Arimo jijo ire
Bi mi mo jijo ki n gbo momi pon
Ki n maa ba ire ose a lo
Baba Sade kanlekun ayo

Egbe
Baba rere silekun ayo mi
O ke ni ji rubi
O ke ni ke eko na lona
O ke ni fi gba Ologun oru bomi mu
Baba rere silekun ayo mi
Emi kan lekun ayo
Adumaradan kan lekun ayo
Iwo ni mo ba i'lo
Mi o ni ba oluya lo
O koju si mi
O dabi obitun nii
O keyin si mi
O dabi asese la orirun
Emi je omo owa
Me i sun ona agbode
Ti mi kii ba se omo owa
Emi iba lo sun enu odi
Emi lomo Emeso ori egun
Eso mu gbogbo ara re'ni
Eso ile wumi
Ti ona oje wu mi
Eso ule mi lo wumi le nii.

I am the offspring of rock-ordained two chieftains
The rock that bears Edemo in my home.
I would accompanmy the child bearer
I wouldn't go with the unfortunate one
He who can dance would go to Ose grove
He who cannot would go too
If I can't dance I would mount my child on my back
And proceed to Ose festival
Sade's father knocks at the door of joy
Benevolent father, open the door of my joy
You will not wake up to meet misfortune
You wouldn't meet the malevolent on the way
You wouldn't drink with the epileptic calabash.
Benevolent father, open the door of my joy
I knock the door of joy
The black and beauty knocks at the door of joy.
It is you I go with
I wouldn't go with the unfortunate one.

You who face me and look like a bride
You back me
You look like the rising sun
I am an offspring of the throne
I don't sleep at the lobby
If I am not an offspring of the throne
I would have slept at the gate.
I am the offspring of warrior on the rock,
Warrior that shows body attractions.
The home warrior attracts me.
That of the Oje road attracts me.
The warrior of my house is the one that
attracts me today.

Although the above poem is intended to shower encomiums on her husband, the poet starts by invoking her own ancestry. She introduces herself as one from a royal birth. She, however, puts her emphasizes on the sense of justice that is prevalent in her community: whether or not you can dance, the Ose festival welcomes you! In the traditional sense, everybody, old and young, is expected to participate in this festival, which is an important religious ritual in the community. She is also happy that she has her own child and can go to the festival carrying her child on her back. The poem shows her happiness with her husband who from every indication has been a responsible father for their child. She calls him "Sade's father." Apart from using this to indicate that he is a good father, she also shows the general Yoruba respect tradition where husband and wife call each other through the name of their children rather than in first name (Baba Onikepe—Onikepe's father; Mama Asabi—Asabi's mother).

The two poems cited above explore very rich language to present sociopolitical issues of domestic relationships. The frequent uses of "child of" and "offspring of" are indications of strong reliance on lineage history as a background for their societal behavior. The Yoruba people place a great value on a good family name. Every individual draws from the fountain of family pride and owes his or her success to the overall glory and name of the family and the community. Jean-Jacques Rousseau's idea of individualism would have no place in Yoruba tradition. Expressing what has come to be the Western heritage of "aloneness" since the later part of eighteenth century, Rousseau says in his *Confessions*:

Myself alone! I know the feelings of my heart, and I know men.
I am not made like any of those I have seen; I venture to believe
that I am not made like any of those who are in existence. If I am

not better, at least I am different. Whether Nature has acted rightly or wrongly in destroying the mould in which she cast me, can only be decided after I have been read. (*The Norton Anthology* 1630)

The philosophy of "Myself alone" would be resisted with all vehemence among the Yoruba. Even though they subscribe to the belief that every person's "Ori," head, is his or her own personal or unique god, every "ori" is invoked from the roots of one's birth and remains connected to one's ancestry. The Yoruba person cannot, therefore, say that he or she is not made like "those who are in existence." He has to constantly draw from wisdom of the elders and the ancestors, to understand the past and forge ahead into the future. A popular traditional Yoruba homage poem goes thus:

nise ni won ranmi wa,
emi ki mo ran ara mi o.
Ni se ni won ran mi wa,
emi ki mo ran ara mio.
Iba mi dowo Mama mi to ranmi wa ile aye

I was sent on an errand to the world
I did not bring myself to this earth.
I was sent on an errand to the world
I did not bring myself to this earth.
My homage goes to my mother who sent me on an errand to this
    earth.

(my translation from Yoruba to English)

Our next example of "domestic political poetry" is also from among the housewives. It involves co-wives who have come to hate each other. The senior wife sees the junior one has an unfit wife for her husband having divorced a previous husband due to what she considers as greed and impatience. In Yoruba culture, divorce is not frequent because the extended families of both husband and wife always intervene and settle rifts in the families. The society frowns at a divorce whether initiated by a man or a woman. The woman, as mother, is always encouraged to stay in the marriage for the sake of her children, since it is believed that any divorce often affects the children more drastically because one person alone may not be able to cater adequately for them. So this woman has divorced one husband and is married to another. The senior wife in the second marriage sings at the tip of her voice so that all the people in the household can hear her:

Laarin Obirin ile
Won o ni fimi sawaari
A f'oogun f'oko ma fi fami o
A f'oogun f'oko ma fi fami o
Ile lo ba mi emi ni'yale
Oni bata gogoro mafi te mi o
Oni bata gogoro ma fi te mi o
Adagba koko wa pale mo o
Ile lo ba mi emi ni'yale
Adagba koko wa pale mo o.

In the midst of women in the house,
I wouldn't be missing,
You who enchant husbands, don't (use juju to) magnetize me
You who enchant husbands, don't magnetize me.
It's in the household you met me, I'm the senior
It's in the household you met me, I'm the senior.
Owner of high-heel shoes, don't step on me
It's in the household you met me, I'm the senior
Owner of high-heel shoes, don't step on me.
Older-woman divorcee, come clear the table
It's in the house you met me, I'm the senior
Older-woman divorcee, [I said] clear the table!

It is clear that a domestic war has been declared in this household, and someone has to make peace between the two sides. Often the husband is responsible for doing so, especially if he still wants to continue to remain polygamous. This type of cases might be presented to a woman leader of the compound, often the eldest wife in the extended family who calls a group of elderly women in the compound to a meeting to make peace between the parties. There may never be a permanent peace until the husband himself knows his politics well and plays it as he assures both wives of his love and respect and ensures that they trust him to maintain equality between them. It is clear the senior wife has several cases against her husband and against the older woman junior wife who she also suspects to possess evil powers. What is more interesting here is the medium she uses to state her case. Poetry is the medium for grumbling and complaints just as it is the medium for encomiums and adoration. I have seen mothers who use poetry to complain about the unbecoming attitude of their grown-up children, and the children who on hearing their mothers sang immediately went on their knees to apologize to their parents!

Perhaps, no oral poet in the whole of Nigeria was and is, still years after Odolaye's death, as blunt, brave, and bold as the Ilorin oral singer,[2] Odolaye Aremu. Not even Mamman Shata Katsina, Dan Maraya Jos, and Haruna na Huje among the Hausas nor Oliver Deque, Ikenga Super, Raggana Ottah, and Agwu Risky among the Igbos are comparable to Odolaye Aremu in political partisanship and in bravery and bluntness in oral performance.

The Yoruba people in Ilorin, Ogbomosho, Oyo, Ibadan, Mushin, Lagos, Ilesha, Ede, Iwo, Ikirun, Saki cities of Nigeria single out Odolaye for special mention when discussing traditional oral griots. Odolaye's feat in traditional oral poetry satisfies what Kofi Anyidoho describes as the art of mythmaking and mythbreaking in traditional art. The art of "mythmaking and mythbreaking" is fundamental to the preoccupation of traditional oral artists in Africa,[3] and Odolaye created myths on issues and around personalities and, conversely, also broke lots of mythical masques shielding many people.

This chapter examines the political feats achieved by Odolaye and how contemporary Yoruba Community in Nigeria relates to him.

Odolaye and his Yoruba audience

Odolaye is one poet whom many Yorubas, right from his Ilorin home, love to hate and hate to love. His songs dominated many political scenes in Nigeria for many years. It is not an exaggeration to say that no oral poet was and, still, is his match in the entire Yoruba community. Haruna Ishola, Yusuf Olatunji, Olarewaju Adepoju, Batuli Alake, Tunbosun Oladapo, Alabi Ogundepo, Oladare Foyanmu, Asana Abake, Ayinla Omowura, Salawa Abeni, Jaigbade Alao, all thrive as pan-Yoruba oral artists. None of them, however, can beat his/her chest in front of Odolaye when it comes to partisan politics and the ability to speak and damn the consequences. Odolaye (now deceased) asserted to me during an interview in the late 1980s that he was never under anybody's tutelage. Political enthusiasts have hailed, encouraged, and even axed this oral poet at different times in contemporary Nigerian history. We will discuss examples of this later.

Despite the degree of popularity and respect this poet enjoys in community circles of his Ilorin and indeed Yoruba homes, he was hardly invited to perform in ceremonies like marriage and naming in the main Ilorin township when he was alive. However, during his lifetime, Yoruba politicians patronized him more than they did other oral poets, and no other Yoruba poet has enjoyed that kind of patronage since Odolaye's death. However, being seen mainly as a politician poet did not limit the scope of Odolaye's songs to only political matters.

Although people seem to have reached a consensus during his lifetime on Odolaye's poetry and thus seemed to have classified his songs as political poetry, my analysis in this chapter shall prove that Odolaye's performance themes and pyrotechnics cut across different themes, even while he was better known as a poet-politician.

My research has shown that the Yoruba people have different reasons for their divergent attitudes toward Odolaye and his poetry. For example, he is loved in some quarters for his originality and humor. Some enthusiasts say Odolaye's voice alone makes them laugh. Yet to others he is too blunt and crudely impolite. Many people even call him "Éléèke èebu—one whose mouth is a house of insults."[4] It is a popular belief that Odolaye in his songs insults even those he praises. I personally prefer him to other local poets on political matters because of his constant agitation for a united Nigeria.

Many Yoruba politicians detested Odolaye during his lifetime. During the political crisis in southwestern Nigeria in the first republic, they called him a rebel against the Yoruba race. They asserted that he did not support any cause of the Yorubas. That he was against the late Chief Obafemi Awolowo, a foremost Yoruba politician and the first premier of the then Nigerian Western Region. These people accused Odolaye of often inciting one Yoruba politician against the other. They insisted that he fueled an air of discord even among the Yoruba Obas.[5] However, his poetry, as we shall begin to see, show that while it may be true that he was harsh on and impatient with those he disagreed with, he certainly loved his country so much. One may safely say that he was a rebel only against those who, in his judgment, were opposed to the cause for Nigerian unity.

Odolaye's artistic philosophy

Excerpts from Odolaye's many songs would reveal that his poetic periscope gazes farther than mere ethnocentric setting. Odolaye was an avowed federalist and promoted politics played within a national structure of a federation. My first example is a song he addressed to all Nigerians, advocating unity and mutual understanding among the ethnically and religiously polarized nation:

> Eyin oselu aye, emaa ma je o ba jee
> Tori ojo tin pa'gun bo ojo ti pe
> Eje ka takaka ka ronu
> Eje ka sowo wa po
> Ki kini ohun le daa o
> An sunle'nan, an be'yan lori
> Olohun o ni je a ri irue ma![6]

Oh you politicians of this world,
    don't destabilize the world
For, the rain has been beating hard on the vulture for so long!
Let's sleep on our backs and think
Let's join hands together
So that our situation can improve
Burning of houses, beheading of people,
May God Almighty put a stop to them!

Nigeria, here, is the metaphorical vulture, which the poet says has been over beaten by the heavily descending rain. The irony is that the "rain," a reference to oppression, repression, instability, and poverty during colonization, is certainly an abnormality here. The rain of colonization and now neo-colonization and globalization, according to Odolaye, has come to destroy and to maim. It rains pebbles and rocks on the vulture who is both naked and homeless. Odolaye admonishes the politicians to desist from being thugs or using thugs and other destructive elements on each other. They must come together to build Nigeria—the vulture. In a Yoruba saying, it is said that *Gunugun kii ku l'ewe, a sai darugbo*, meaning "The vulture never dies young. It grows to be old." Odolaye implores every Nigerian politician in every community, and in every local and state government areas, to make a hecatomb of their differences and to consolidate their gains for the sake of a strong Nigeria. In the next song, he declares a similar challenge to Nigerian politicians:

Eyin 'joba eko, e maa ma je o baje
Ijoba Ibadan, e maa ma je o bajee
Ijoba Oyo, e maa ma je o bajee
Oselu Ogbomosho, e maa ma je o bajee
Oselu Kuwara, e maa ma je o bajee
Oselu Sokoto, e maa ma je o bajee
Oselu Kaduna, e maa ma je o bajee
Igbomina, e maa ma je o bajee
Oselu Ile-Ife, e maa ma je o bajee
Eje ka so'wopo k'aye o d'okan o![7]

You (who form the) Government of Eko [Lagos], save her (Nigeria)
    from destruction
Government of Ibadan, save her from destruction
Government of Oyo, save her from destruction
Politicians of Ogbomoso, save her from destruction
Politicians of Kwara, save her from destruction
Politicians of Sokoto, save her from destruction

Politicians of Kaduna, save her from destruction
Igbomina, save her from destruction
Politicians of Ile-Ife, save her from destruction
Let us join hands and make the world one!

Odolaye's preachments are quite pragmatic. The "world" in the last line refers to Nigeria. Although literally one may think it is naïve to expect the "world" to be one and united, what he wanted here was a unity of purpose and love for growth, peace, and progress of Nigeria. His was not a postprandial oratory. He wailed and wailed that Nigeria must not be destroyed. The geographical distribution of the Nigerian peoples and the governments the poet appealed to testify to his nationalistic outlook. For example, Oyo, Ogbomosho, and Ibadan are Yoruba communities in Western Nigeria. Kaduna and Sokoto are Hausa/Fulani in the northern part of the country. Odolaye, in another song, wants all Nigerians to reason together and to show love:

Eje ka takaka, ka ro'nu
Eje ka ni'fe ara wa
Eranti awon ota
Ti won d'enu erin le![8]

Let's sleep on our backs, and think!
Let's love ourselves!!
[Let's] remember the enemies,
They are set at making a mockery of us.

The "adversaries" Odolaye had in mind are those who, within and without the country, believed that Nigeria could not survive after its independence from Great Britain in 1960. Odolaye felt that those enemies were eager to see that the country disintegrated so that they could mock the self-rule seekers. Odolaye enjoined Nigerians to love one another and to try to shame the detractors.

The poet rarely sang without touching on issues bothering on national unity and survival. He would wail often during his performance: "Naijiriya!"—Nigeria! He often paid homage to many past Nigerian leaders, Azikiwe, Balewa, Bello, Aguiyi Ironsi, Akintola, and Adelabu, who gained independence for Nigeria while also challenging contemporary leaders to prove their worth to Nigeria by developing the country.

Odolaye commented regularly on the sociopolitical and economic activities in Ilorin, his home community, and indeed in the entire

Kwara State to which Ilorin is the capital city. He was always very bold at putting forward bold suggestions to solving the community's problem. For example, when the then governor of Kwara State, Adamu Atta, quarreled with the then senate leader of the Nigerian Senate, Olusola Saraki, his political godfather who represented Ilorin-Asa senatorial district in the Nigerian Senate, Odolaye, employed his poetry for a reconciliatory role. He sang repeatedly at the climax of that feud:

Amon edakun e ro wo!
B'erin meji ba n ja ni'nu igbo,
Aaaa, koko, eruwa, gbogbo igi inu igbe oo
Lara o man ta
Eyin eeyan jankan-jankan,
Dokita Saraki, Sulu Gambari, Akanbi Oniyangi,
Adamu Atta,
Kilo se tee le perayin jo
Kee ba'rayin soro,
Ki gbogbo Kwara o toro,
Ka ma rije, ka ri mu, ka ma rale, kamaa kole
Ki oni kaluku o maa tun aye baba re se.[9]

But please, have a thought!
When two elephants fight in the forest,
Haaa! grasses, every tree in the bush
Shall feel pain on its body!!
All you big, big people:
Doctor Saraki, Sulu Gambari, Akanbi Oniyangi, Adamu Atta,
Why can't you call yourselves together
And talk (truth) to yourselves!
So that we could have (enough) to eat, to drink,
to buy land, to build houses
So that everyone can develop his father's place.

Odolaye's words here may be soft, but they are certainly direct and straight to the point! They are satires that project the stark failures of the quarreling leaders. The poet challenged them to have some thoughts. He reminded them that their conflicting egos caused the masses, those he called "grasses" and "every tree in the bush," untold sufferings. Odolaye reinstated that abundant food and shelter could only be available to people at peace times. The poet asked the leaders to reconcile so that no community would suffer.

Unlike most traditional singers in Africa, Odolaye did not stop at mere verbal agitation. The general belief that professional oral artists would lose important patronage if they become partisans did not bother him. He felt that an oral poet with a deepest sense of responsibility need not be a political and social prostitute. He carefully chose his tent and abided patriotically by it. He held strongly to the view that every poet must have an ideology or principle in line with his/her poetic vision and must stick solidly to it. He believed that it was the only way the society could respect the poet.

During the first republic in Nigeria, from 1962 to 1966, Odolaye associated with the Northern Peoples Congress (NPC), which controlled the central government. In the second republic, 1979 to 1983, the poet publicly declared for the National Party of Nigeria (NPN), which also eventually won the presidential election, secured the highest number of gubernatorial seats in the Nigerian federation and controlled the federal government. While declaring for the NPN, Odolaye sang:

> Baba mi daakun,
> N o s'onile
> Gbogbo egbon mi,
> N o s'onile,
> Gbogbo Eko
> N o s'onile,
> Egbe Sagari wumi pipo o
> Emi na o maa ni yan'le loodi o.[10]

> Please my father,
> I want to join the (party) with the house symbol.
> You all my elderly ones,
> I want to join the (party) with the house.
> All people of Lagos,
> I want to join the one with the house.
> The party of Shagari is after my heart,
> I won't keep malice with the house!

A symbol of a house was the logo of the defunct NPN. The Yorubas call the party, *Egbe Onile*—"the party with the house symbol." It would be fair to say that Odolaye's concern for a true national unity probably attracted him to that party. It seemed the only political party with a true national spread. For example, apart from winning the presidential election in 1979, the defunct NPN also controlled most of the states, and the highest number of seats at the national Houses of Senate and Representative. In teaming up with the NPN, Odolaye's preoccupation was the oneness of Nigeria. This is evident in some of his songs that became campaign slogans for the NPN in Yoruba areas of the country:

> Igboro Ilorin,
> Waan Najiriya!
> Bo de Kano,
> Waan Najiriya!
> Ni Sokoto,
> Waan Najiriya!
> Kaduna,
> Waan Najiriya[11]

> On the streets of Ilorin,
> One Nigeria!
> If you go to Kano,
> One Nigeria!
> In Sokoto,
> One Nigeria!
> Kaduna,
> One Nigeria ...

The defunct NPN's slogan, "One Nigeria, One Nation, One Destiny," was a very attractive weapon, even if fraudulently, that won the hearts of many nationalist Nigerians to the party.

Although Odolaye was sincere in his concern for national unity and in his thought that a party with a symbol of a house and a slogan of One Nation, One Destiny would gear the country toward a common destiny, the catastrophic end of the second republic in the hands of the NPN, however, proved that Odolaye's (and many other Nigerians') choice was unfortunately mere cosmetic. Though the party had the largest spread, it proved clearly that a national spread did not commensurate with a sincere concern for the majority downtrodden Nigerians! The allegations of election riggings that led into a "landslide victory" of the NPN in 1983 election culminated into the violence of a military coup led by Muhammadu Buhari and Babatunde Idiagbon that brought the second republic democracy into an abrupt end. Yet, it would be extremely difficult to fault the oral poet or any ordinary Nigerian who supported the ruling party because of its nationalistic claims.

Odolaye's political advocations

Odolaye regularly advocated for participatory democracy and insisted that every part of Nigeria must take a vibrant part in the governance of the country. He performed several songs that show that he did not accept a concept that political power in Nigeria should remain with any one particular linguistic, ethnic, or geographical group in Nigeria. The following song, in particular, deals with the issues of power manipulation, monopolization, and drunkenness:

Bi kinihun ba kan wa,
Ema je o baje.
Te ban ranti otun
Bi kinihun ba kan yin,
Ese 'ranti osi.
Ema je kod'awa lowanbe tinbaluje
Ori buruku nin mu k'olori o wajoba maya.[12]

When it (the governance of Nigeria) comes to our turn,
Don't let it (Nigeria) be destroyed
If you remember the right section,
When it comes to your turn,
Remember also the left section
Remember the front, remember the back
Don't let us make governance 'We-are-the-one-in-charge,'
    which spoils a country …
It is a bad head that makes a leader
    wants to monopolize his reign.

In the song, Odolaye asserts that the ruling party has a responsibility to extend hands of fellowship to other political parties and to ensure that the opposition participates actively in governance. In the last line, Odolaye maintains that it is a "bad head," meaning a cursed head, a head destined to fail, "makes a leader to want to monopolize his reign."

Odolaye's uncompromising political stance put him in a minority among the Yoruba people of Nigeria. It sharply set him against many of his traditional audience populations in Lagos, Ibadan, Oyo, and Abeokuta. Odolaye was a strong supporter of Samuel Akintola, the late premier of the then Nigerian Western Region during the first Nigerian republic. He strongly backed Akintola's alliance with the NPC's controlled federal government that Akintola's party, the Action Group (AG), was against.[13]

Odolaye always argued in his songs that Akintola's actions were in the primary interest of the Yoruba people. He saw Akintola's step as a necessity to the survival of the Nigerian nation. This was contradictory to the late Obafemi Awolowo's (the AG leader's) opinion and to those of his teaming Yoruba loyalists, who, together, saw Akintola as a betrayer of the Yoruba race.[14] On the contrary, Odolaye praised Akintola for leading the Yoruba people to the fold of a true national politics and for saving them from a regional, sectional, and myopic political party, which he felt the defunct AG represented. After the assassination of Akintola in 1966, Odolaye smelled a rat in the killing and pointed out the conspiracy of his murder. He sang:

Aso wipe won o mo paa
Won pa
Won p'agbe tan aye o r'aro da ma
Won p'aluko tan aye o r'osun
Won pa lekeleke aye o gbadun efun funfun.
Aso, ani emapa,
E paa
Won pa gunungun aye o r'oju
Won pa'kalamango, aye o raaye[15]

We kept warning that they shouldn't kill him (Akintola)
Yet they killed him
They killed the agbe-bird, and the world could no longer get aro-dye
They killed the aluko-bird and the world could no longer find
    osun-dye
They killed lekeleke-bird, and the world could no longer enjoy
    the efun-dye
We kept saying they shouldn't kill him,
Yet they killed him
They killed the gunnugun bird, and the world is no longer healthy
They killed the akalamago-bird, and the world is no longer stable!

Odolaye believed that Akintola's murder was as a result of a well-hatched plot to destabilize Nigeria. He referred to it as "an unceasing rainfall." The rainfall, ironically again, resulted into a death. According to Odolaye, only God knew the number of people the violence would sweep away. Odolaye insisted:

Ajalaa-gbe nbe lorun osan gangan
Kiya o ma je Yooba lofa sababi e.[16]

Ajalaa-gbe (Akintola) is now in day-light heaven
His struggle to save the Yorubas from suffering caused his death!

Odolaye gave adjudication on the matter to God whom, he says, "knows the true cause of the enmity between the cat and the rat." During the 1979 national election campaigns, radio stations in some Yoruba speaking states of Nigeria used Odolaye's songs as campaign jingles. Indeed, the songs were a winner for the NPN in the nation as a whole: "Olohun lo yan Sagari, Seehu, Sagari,—It is God who has chosen Shagari, Shehu Shagari." However, Odolaye's political enemies multiplied among the Yorubas who actually campaigned and voted *en masse* for the defunct Unity Party of Nigeria (UPN), the party that featured Obafemi Awolowo as its presidential candidate. After the victory of the NPN in the 1979 federal elections that Odolaye had much predicted, the poet went on field performances and on records to celebrate his party's successes. He asked those he called the enemies of his party to see the true writings on the wall and to decamp to the federal ruling party. He directed some of his songs particularly at the people of Ibadan:

Eyin omo Ibadan
Ewa gba f'olohun.
Gbogbo nkan tanwi lo se,
Sagari geri ijoba.[17]

You offsprings of Ibadanland,
Come and surrender to God!
Everything we have said has come to past!
Shagari has ascended the throne!

Rumors had it that many Ibadan people threatened Odolaye's life. His call on them to desert the UPN and join the NPN was considered an insult. Odolaye fled Ibadan for his dear life!

Odolaye's poetry for his patrons

Olusola Saraki[18] and Shehu Shagari enjoyed much patronage from Odolaye in the second republic. Odolaye played the same role for these two politicians as a Ghanaian legendary griot played for Kwame Nkrumah, former president of Ghana. According to Kwesi Yankah in an article, "The Making and Breaking of Kwame Nkrumah: The Role of Oral Poetry,"[19] Nkrumah's poet, Okyeame Boafo Akuffo, composed heavily patronizing songs that boosted Nkrumah's image and made the leader ever present in the lives of Ghanaians. Nkrumah, with the power of Akuffo's poetry, almost became the idol of worship for most Ghanaians. One nickname created around Nkrumah by the poet, "Osagyfo" (savior-at-war), replaced the state constitutional title of president! In the same way, Odolaye Aremu's poetry for Saraki and Shagari swelled their political images. To the people of Ilorin, for example, Saraki became a synonym of Shagari and vice versa, and both names became larger than life. Odolaye nicknamed Saraki as, "Ojo Weliweli Kuwara," that is, "the showering rain of Kwara"! Saraki soon became nationally tagged and acknowledged as "the strong man of Kwara Politics":

Dokita Saraki Oloye Baba Bukola
Ojo weliweli Kwara
O ti su bayi
O to n ro bayi
Eyin o rii ni,
Bo ti n de mekunu ti de'joba,
Okan soso to n toju gbogbo Ilu
Omo Mutahiru ...
Owo Saraki koja an wadi,
Owo Saraki koja a n saagun
Owo naa to se'joba
Olohun lo fun.[20]

Doctor Saraki, the titled chief, father of Bukola,
The showering rain of Kwara:
It is cloudy now
It is raining!
Don't you see,
How it soothes both the governed and the governors,
The only person who takes care of a whole town
The offspring of Mutahiru ...
The wealth of Doctor Saraki is beyond probe
The wealth of Saraki is beyond magic
That wealth is enough for governance (of a country)!
It is Allah that gives him!!

Odolaye in addressing the issue of Saraki's wealth warned that it was beyond any probe because, according to him, it was Allah—God—that gave Saraki the riches. Odolaye created a kind of myth around Saraki. Several Ilorin people decades after in the twenty-first century would still swear that Saraki's wealth flows like the waters of the Atlantic Ocean!

However, soon after Shagari was declared as the president-elect in the 1979 Nigerian election, Odolaye composed a song to advise him:

Haji Shehu Shagari,
Ti won ba ni o d'owo re, gbogbo oro Nijiriya
So fun won wipe od'owo Olohun
Oba min adigun ajoko d'eke n masalaasi[21]

Haji Shehu Shagari,
If people say all depend on you, every matter in Nigeria,
Say (to them): 'everything depends on God!'
My God, Adigun, is He who catches the deceitful even in the mosque!

Odolaye wanted Shagari to realize that he could not succeed on his own! He admonished him to be honest, to seek God's guidance and the support of other politicians. This is the nature of patriotic partisanship of Odolaye, the poet. The last line of the above song is a warning that anyone who cheats or deceives others would face the wrath of God, even if, as a Muslim, such a person shows excessiveness in his or her worship of God by performing the Islamic *salat* (ritual prayers) nonstop until he or she falls down and dies in the mosque!

Many more politicians benefited from Odolaye's poetry. Like I explained earlier, nearly all the past and the present Nigerian leaders regularly had one thing or the other performed for them by Odolaye. For example, after Olusegun Obasanjo's military regime handed over power to civilian administration in 1979, Odolaye commented on Obasanjo's actions:

Agbadun Obasanjo pupo,
Obasanjo, ooko isomo ni n man omo lara
Agbadun Obasanjo,
Ee ri gbogbo Naijiriya ti to, ti gbogbo re ndun yin!
O ni laakayi pupo, o lopolo pupo,
Ko fi'gba kan bo kan ninu.[22]

We enjoyed Obasanjo very well
Obasanjo, the name given to a child is what fits the child

We enjoyed Obasanjo
Can't you see that the whole of Nigeria is peaceful and very sweet!
He is very brilliant, he is very intelligent,
He does not put one calabash into the other!

Obviously, Obasanjo's peaceful handover of power to the civilian government in 1979 impressed Odolaye. The last line in the above song is a literal translation from its original Yoruba version, "Fi'gba kan bo kan ni nun," "putting one calabash into another calabash," means being dubious in Yoruba expression. Odolaye proclaimed Obasanjo as honest and just.

Odolaye and his attacks on his foes

Odolaye defines enmity as a disagreement on both social and political principles. Several of Odolaye's songs are sharp attacks on those who do not share his political thought. He severely rebuked some sets of people whom he believed were unjust and unfit for leadership positions in the society. In one instance, Odolaye sings:

Aye fele fele, Aye fee le lu kan raa won,
Iya si nje omo elomii bii ko jade laye
Ama awon Olosi eyan, kara nbani eyan, omo ale eyan,
Won se b'olohun go ni,
Oba tii dani tan tii duro ti ni
Allahu Rabbi tii duro tini nigba eru ba fe wo.[23]

The world is very light, almost (capable of being) torned apart.
Some people suffer as if they should quit the world
But some stupid people, useless people, idiot people,
They think God is senseless:
Allahu Rabbi (my God) who stays by one when one's burden is
    getting unbearable!

Those whom Odolaye calls "stupid" and "useless" people here are the oppressors who constantly exploit the downtrodden masses for their own selfish ends. He implies in the songs that such cheats use religion and other spiritual powers to justify their inimical acts. Odolaye, however, insisted that God was on the side of the oppressed. Odolaye also attacked his patrons' adversaries. He seemed to take up the fight that we might regard as his patrons' fights.[24]

Odolaye and the legitimacy for his poetic preoccupation

Odolaye Aremu often insisted that he did not praise or condemn people just for the sake of the exercise. He asserted that individual person's activities in the society determined the songs he composed for that individual. In a record he released in December 1990 on EMI label and titled "Olowe Mowe," the poet attempted to clear himself of double-dealing. He sang:

> Odolaye Aremu,
> Aja kwara ti kii gbo lasan
> Bio ba r'eran
> Asi r'eeyan!
> B'eyan o daa,
> Aa ni po daa,
> B'eyan o suhan,
> Aa ni po suhan,
> Awa na o maa ni f'igbakan bo kan n nu.[25]

> Odolaye Aremu,
> The dog of Kwara who doesn't bark without a cause
> If he hasn't seen a goat,
> He must have seen a human being!
> If a person isn't good,
> We won't say he is good
> If a person isn't decent,
> We won't say he is decent,
> We too would never put one calabash into another!

Odolaye is in a way reemphasizing what Chidi Amuta says about the basic preoccupation of an African poet in his community:

> In the African world, this historical necessity, in which the poet as a man of culture devotes his art and life to the pursuit of justice and freedom, has become part of the very legitimacy of the poetic undertaking.[26]

Thus, Odolaye is very conscious of his poetic direction and is already declaring literally that he was the "dog" keeping guard on Kwara State, like the police dog, the night watchman's dog—going after thieves! The "goat" and the "human being" referred to in Odolaye's songs are the metaphorical thieves whom the police or the watchman's dogs give some chase. By implication, Odolaye was out to pursue those he sees as thieves and unjust in the entire Nigerian society. But to what extent could we trust Odolaye's judgment on who was a thief and was unjust among our political leaders in Nigeria? Whether we trust Odolaye's judgment or not in identifying society's thieves and cheats, one thing one can be sure about is his poetic honesty.

Odolaye and artistic beauty

It is easy to assume, especially in the light of our discussion so far, that this great poet's sole commitment was to politics. He was, however, equally committed to excellence of the creative arts as a commitment to the African aesthetics of an art for the sake of life does not lead to neglect in the use of excellent skills in wedding together masterpieces of artistic language and sociocultural content. He was one *Dàdàkúàdá* poet who stuck to the oldest performance techniques in the poetic genre. For example, he adopted and retained the simultaneous delivery technique and the talking-level technique which dominated the first stage of *Dàdàkúàdá*'s development.[27] Under the simultaneous delivery technique, Odolaye and one or more artists sang simultaneously. In the talking-level technique, he resorted to a talking-level discussion to explain one issue or the other. Other *Dàdàkúàdá* poets use mainly the call and response technique.[28] Odolaye's songs are heavily loaded with dazzling proverbs, idioms, hyperboles, metaphors, and lexical matches. We can observe many of these usages in several songs already cited in this chapter. The intensity of hyperboles in Odolaye's compositions also makes his art unique. This is one reason some of his fans still regard him as the king of humor. For example, while praising one Alao Gbede in Ilorin, Odolaye sang:

Too ba de Ita Aburo
E lo wo masalasi Alao Gbede to ko
Ee se bi ede Madina ni
Yaarasula llahi!
Eni to ba kirun ni bi Masalasi taa wi yi,
Nita Aburo, Masalasi Alao Gbede,
Ina Olohun d'eewo fun.[29]

If you get to Ita-aburo, in Ilorin,
At the mosque of Alao Gbede,
The one he built,
You will think you have reached Madina (Saudi Arabia).
Whoever prays in that mosque,

In Aburo area, the mosque of Alao Gbede,
The hell of God is forbidden for him.

It is not only the poetic claim that Gbede's mosque is like Madina, a holy city in Saudi Arabia, that amuses us, but also the assertion that whoever prays in this mosque would enter God's paradise! Would this be true even if such a person had committed murder? Imagine again Odolaye's often sang that "Though God is everywhere, He sleeps in Ilorin"! The poet is only appealing to the audience's sense of humor. He started his 1990 album with the songs:

The owner of a proverb knows his proverb
The song of Aremu knows whom it is referring to.[30]

Another very unique thing about Odolaye's poetry was his drumming pattern. Like his songs, his beats are very fast. It is the *Pami-Oduku* pattern. Most other *Dàdàkúàdá* artists prefer *Woro* pattern, which is slower and requires majestic movements during dancing. One needs to be really agile to dance to Odolaye's fast beats.[31]

Conclusion

That Odolaye's preoccupations have always been the unity of Nigeria are beyond contention. Given the present postcolonial realities of ethnic hatred, injustice, oppression, inequality, and corruption in Nigeria as a whole, an important duty might still be to ask whether traditional oral poetry would serve as an effective medium to propagate the country's unity? Can a traditional poet who depends on his or her patrons' patronage for survival be effectively and responsibly partisan in a poverty-ridden society like Nigeria? Was Odolaye Aremu, in particular, successful in these endeavors?

Amilcar Carbral[32] discusses the dialectical potential of traditional culture. Like him, I believe that it is the commercialization and the bastardization of traditional art in contemporary Africa that seemed to have taken it out of politics. The traditional public poet, the palace poet, and even the religious griots of traditional Africa are deeply into politics. They never separate politics from art. What I believe Odolaye has done, therefore, was to insist on keeping the traditional function of African art. The question of the Nigerian unity is a political one and cannot be divorced from a true political discourse. Nigerian politicians and civil organizations called for a Sovereign National Conference. The post-2000 Obasanjo regime, which had rejected the earlier call for a national conference, suddenly sponsored a national political dialogue, which was later found to be a strategy to perpetuate Obasanjo in power in a bid to change the Nigerian Constitution to give himself a third term in office as President of Nigeria. Indeed, a different Obasanjo from 1979, now wanted the National Assembly to change the constitution so that he could go for a third term in office! Yet, Odolaye was honest in praising Obasanjo's initial action of handing over power to civilian regime in 1979 and had no way of knowing that the same Obasanjo would resort to diabolical acts aimed at manipulating his way into a third term in office as a civilian president in 2007!

Nigerian oral poets like Odolaye have never ceased to play their roles in promoting political dialogues in Nigeria. They constantly participated in mobilizing Nigerians against government's excesses. Odolaye chose to remain attached to what can be described as a peasant or a poor man's aesthetics, that is, the course of politics and partisanship in art. Yet, we must observe that unfortunately postcolonial realities of poverty and neglect of traditional values might have weakened the strength of Odolaye's partisanship. There is constantly a contradiction between efforts to preach the Nigerian unity, fight for ordinary people, and the roles to please wealthy patrons, who are now the rich and corrupt lords of postindependent Nigeria.

Chidi Amuta hints at what he calls the two "tribes" of poets: those who use their arts "to legitimize, uphold and advance the cause of the status quo ..." and those who use their talents "to challenge the ruling class and thus champion the cause of those who bear the burden of oppression."[33] My discussion of Odolaye's oral art definitely shows that he cared for the poor masses. But evidence also showed that he sang for, and sometimes in his poetic exuberance over-promoted the oppressive rich lords. In the songs he composed in March 1993, Odolaye showered encomiums on Sha'aba Lafiagi, the then civilian governor of Kwara State.[34] He claimed that Sha'aba had ensured an uninterrupted electric power supply in Ilorin. This statement was not only a fallacy but disrespectful of the intelligence of the people that he sang for. This is hardly what a traditional oral poet does in Africa, and I have no reason to believe that Odolaye was out to deceive the ordinary people. It was true that electricity supply throughout Ilorin and indeed the entire nation, during and after Sha'aba's regime, was regularly irregular. NEPA,[35] the sole generator and distributor of public electricity in Ilorin, was a federal government board and was never under the authority of Kwara State Government. Therefore, the governor could have been able to only slightly influence its performance. Although Sha'aba was a civilian governor, the federal government was under the military head of state, Ibrahim Babangida and the federal control was still characteristically dictatorship. Yet, Odolaye must have got his story from Sha'aba Lafiagi's lieutenants who are anxious for Odolaye to portray their leader in a better light. Perhaps, one weakness in the traditional oral poet is that sometime in collecting information about a patron, they could fall in the hands of those who might deceive them by giving them false information. In this case, Odolaye might have relied on paid agents of Sha'aba Lafiagi.

Poets like Odolaye must continue to fight personal poverty and to meet survival challenges in their contemporary communities. They cannot afford to undermine their artistic preoccupation by throwing their responsibility as society's keepers overboard. Traditional African poets can retain their positions as true poor people spokespersons if, even while still being partisan, they first defend the true sociopolitical, economic, and moral stance of their people and are cautious in rushing to offer their oral art to promoting politicians. They must limit encomiums on contemporary rich and "global" lords and political leaders. They must stop exaggerating the so-called qualities and achievements of politicians. Indeed, these are strong ethics for all traditional oral poets in contemporary African societies of our global century.

Notes

1 Bayo Ogunjimi and Abdul-Rasheed Na'Allah, *Introduction to African Oral Literature and Performance* (Trenton, NJ: Africa World P (AWP), 2005). 2005 revision and expansion by A. Na'Allah.

2 Read about the origin, development, and artists of Dàdàkúádá, the Ilorin traditional oral poetry in Abdul-Rasheed Na'Allah, "Dàdàkúádá: Origin, Artists and Performance Techniques of an Ilorin Oral Art," in *Nigeria Magazine*, 56.1, 2 (1988): 26–36.

3 See the chapter on "Oral Tradition, Islamic Culture and Topicality in the Songs of Mamman Shata Katsina and Omoekee Amao Ilorin." See also Kofi Anyidoho, "Mythmaker and Mythbreaker: The Oral Poet as Earwitness" in *African Literature in Its Social and Political Dimensions*. Ed. Eileen Julien et al. (Washington: African Literature Association and Three Continents P, Inc., 1983): 5–14; Kofi Anyidoho, "Realism in Oral Narrative Performance," in *Acta Ethnographica Academiae Scientiarum Hungaricae*, 34.1–34.4 (1986–1988): 49–63. These papers show that oral poets' involvement in politics, as the present work tries to show among the Yorubas with the Odolaye example, is an agelong African tradition.

4 This view is held especially in his Ilorin home. Everyone I interviewed claimed this.

5 An "Oba" is the traditional ruler of a Yoruba community. People easily make references to several songs in which Odolaye praised some Obas, that is, the Alafin of Oyo, Olubadan of Ibadan, and Owa Obokun of Ijesaland, who have been on very strong antagonism to the Ooni of Ife on the question of superiority in and chairmanship of the then Oyo State

Traditional Council. Oyo state was split into two separate states, Oyo and Osun, in 1991, by the Babangida administration.

6 Odolaye Aremu, "Elenini Aye." Ariyo Sound ASSLP 058 B, 1979. All translations into English of Yoruba songs cited in this paper are mine.

7 Ibid.

8 Ibid., "Esalo Fa'ye." Olatunbosun Records ORCLP 151 A, 1982.

9 Ibid.

10 Odolaye, 058 B 1979.

11 Ibid., "Shehu Shagari Geri Ijoba." Ariyo Sound ASSLIP 058 A, 1979.

12 Ibid.

13 Read the full story on this matter in Victor Ladipo, *Akintola: the Man and the Legend* (Enugu: Delta of Nigeria, 1982).

14 Today, there is a kind of notorious (rather rebellious) weed in Yoruba land of Nigeria called "koko Akintola." This weed is so named because it gives farmers lots of problems. Read *Akintola: the Man* for a full story of how and why some Yoruba alleged that this former Premier of the Western region was a betrayer of the Yorubas.

15 Odolaye "Iku Akintola." Olatunbosun Records.

16 Ibid.

17 Ibid., ASSLP 058 A, 1979.

18 Saraki represented the Ilorin-Asa-Moro Senatorial district at the National House of Senate and was the senate leader between 1979 and 1983.

19 Kwesi Yanka, "The Making and Breaking of Kwame Nkrumah: the Role of Oral Poetry" in *African Literature in Its Social and Political Dimensions*. Ed. Eileen Julien et al. (Washington: Three Continents P, 1986): 15–21.

20 Odolaye, "Shehu Shagari Geri Ijoba."

21 Ibid., ASSLP 058A, 1979.

22 Ibid., ASSLP 058B, 1979.

23 Ibid., "E saalo f'ye." ORCLP 151A, 1982.

24 This is one of the terrible effects of the bourgeoisie on traditional arts. Just for the money they offer them, modern oral poets become spokesmen of their patrons, fighting their fights on their behalf. See A. Na'Allah, "African Literature and Poscoloniality: Projections into the Twenty First Century," in *Canadian Review of Comparative Literature*, 22.3 (1995): 569–585.

25 Odolaye, "Olowe Mowe." NEMI 0654B, 1990.

26 Chidi Amuta, *The Theory of African Literature* (London: ZED Books Ltd., 1989): 177.

27 See A. Na'Allah, "*Dàdàkúádá*: Trends in the Development of Ilorin Traditional Oral Poetry." B. A. (Ed.) Thesis, U of Ilorin (1988), for thorough analyses and exemplifications of these and other *Dàdàkúádá*'s performance technics.

28 Ibid., See also "Dàdàkúádá: Origin ..."

29 Odolaye, ASSLP 058A, 1979.

30 Odolaye, "Olowe Mowe," NEMI 0654B, 1990.

31 Read more about Odolaye's drum patterns in "Dàdàkúádá: Trends ..." Chapter 4.

32 Amilcar Cabral, *Return to the Source: Selected Speeches* (London: Monthly Review P, 1973): 177.

33 Amuta, *The Theory*, p. 177.

34 Odolaye, "Ema se gbagbe Oluwa." BMLPS 08A, 1993.

35 NEPA is the acronym for the National Electric Power Authority, now defunct.

7 Aremu Ose and performance topicality

Aremu Ose[1] is a unique Ilorin oral poet in the sense that he deploys a kind of voice that portrays literary power and authority as a Dàdàkúàdá poet. His songs are generally delivered in what I have called the "lead and follow" pattern like Jaigbade Alao and Omoeke Amao. However, unlike these two Dàdàkúàdá poets, Aremu Ose employs a kind of force with every word he sings that sometime a listener may conclude that there are some metaphysical potencies with his songs. It is like a person who is uttering an incantation with a voice of force, which can denote an order that it comes to pass as it is being uttered. There is a song I remember hearing from Aremu Ose which to me makes no semantic sense, but artistic and psychological reality: *oriwo riwowo riwowo gbogbo ara lo kango o, karinkasa!* Well, at the end of the day, "riwowo" makes no semantic sense but gives a clear impression of a great incantatory and cultic power and of a person who has power beyond words that must not be crossed! The clarity in his voice when he sings is another magic of his effectiveness as an oral performer and poet. In this chapter, I like to present some of Ose's topical songs as a singer of social reality. He is not afraid to address any social and political persons. Even when, unlike Odolaye Aremu, a person cannot name Arenu Ose as a politically partisan poet, Ose is the singer of engagement in all its ramifications.

One of his very popular songs is known as "Alikurani Nsoro,"[2] the Qur'an is speaking! Here is how he started this song:

EGBE:	Alkurani nsoro
	Gogbo oni laakaye ni i bawii
BOTO:	Oro ire ni o so jade
EGBE:	Alkurani nsoro
	Oni laakaye nii bawii

AREMU OSE: Bile basu
Eni o gbon, eni o go won a sun lo
Bile bama
Eni o gbon, eni o go won a dide
Okunkun la wa yi oo
Olohun Oba lo le fimale re han gbogbo wa
Gbogbo ise ta a banse
Pelu inu mima

CHORUS: The Qur'an is peaking
All the sensible ones are its target

BOTO: Speech of good tiding is what you should utter

CHORUS: The Qur'an is speaking
The sensible ones are its target

AREMU OSE: When the sun is set
The cleaver one, the dull one, they all go to sleep
When the sun rises, the cleaver one, the dull one, they all wake from sleep
We are now in sunset darkness
Only God Almighty can show us that show us a good sunrise!
Whatever work we do
With one clean mind

Aremu Ose is pretty much equating the message of the oral poet to the message of the Qur'an in terms of saying truth to power. The poet is appealing to people who would use their senses and make necessary changes in their lives! The metaphors of sunrise and sunset, those of going to sleep and waking up, are all intended to demonstrate the many opportunities presented to man, and what we choose and how we do them are human choices: "Whatever work we do/ With one clean mind"! Later in the same song, Aremu Ose addresses issues of hunger and of producing food as farmers:

AREMU OSE: Bonfita Miliki olope
Gaari olooyo
Bi isu bi elubo
Olohun o ni je o won lodede gbogbo wa a
Olohun o ma ma je a lounje nle o
Tori ko si arun ti awon Dokita eewo
Ko wa si Dokita to le wo ebi, afeni to ba lounje[3]

AREMU OSE: Bonvita, Can Milk
Powdered Cassava drink
Food like yam, like yam flower
Oh God don't let them be scares in our houses
Oh God let us have what to eat in our houses
Because there is no sickness that doctor cannot treat
There is no doctor that can treat hunger except those
who have food!

The poet sings about the importance of farming for every part of
Nigeria:

AREMU OSE: Ise Agbe nise ile wa a ni Nanjeriya

BOTO: Akiika ni

AREMU OSE: Ipinle Ondo ema je asole e
Ejaa mura siise

BOTO: Oyaa!

CHORUS: Ipinle Ondo ema je a sole eee
Eje a mura siisee

AREMU OSE: Ipinle Ogun ema je asole e
Eje a mura siisee

CHORUS: Ipinle Ogun ema je asolee
Eje a mura siise

AREMU OSE: Ipinle midu-weesi, ema je asole
Eje a mura siise

CHORUS: Ipinle midu-wesi ema je asole
Eje a mura siisee

AREMU OSE: Ipinle Oyo ema je asole
Eje a mura siise

CHORUS: Ipinle Oyo ema je asole
Eje a mura siise

AREMU OSE: Ipinle Kuwara ema je asole
Eje a mura siise

CHORUS: Ipinle Kuwara ema je asole
Eje a mura siise![4]

AREMU OSE: Farming is the profession of our country
BOTO: It is the truth!
AREMU OSE: Ondo State don't let us be lazy
              Let us work hard (on the farm)!
CHORUS: Ondo State don't let us be lazy
              Let us work hard (on the farm)!
AREMU OSE: Ogun State don't let us be lazy
              Let us work hard (on the farm)!
CHORUS: Ogun State don't let us be lazy
              Let us work hard (on the farm)!
AREMU OSE: Midwest State don't let us be lazy
              Let us work hard (on the farm)!
CHORUS: Midwest State don't let us be lazy
              Let us work hard (on the farm)!
AREMU OSE: Oyo State don't let us be lazy
              Let us work hard (on the farm)!
CHORUS: Oyo State don't let us be lazy
              Let us work hard (on the farm)!
AREMU OSE: Kwara State don't let us be lazy
              Let us work hard (on the farm)!
CHORUS: Kwara State don't let us be lazy
              Let us work hard (on the farm)!

The singer covers all states in Nigeria and admonishes them to take farming more seriously! I like to discuss another song which I have reproduced elsewhere,[5] but which I had not taken an opportunity to discuss in any detail. I will be failing if I ignore the opportunity this book presents because as far as I am concerned that song seems to me the bravest and most daunting opportunity taken by Aremu Ose in his performance of topical poetry. He addresses the then president of Nigeria and passes a clear judgment on him that his administration has failed. In my view, no one can discuss Aremu Ose's topical poetry without revisiting this one song. Still addressing the issue of hunger and out-of-reach commodities by the poor, he approaches Chief Olusegun Obasanjo, as the sitting president, and demands for a change in policy regarding food importation to Nigeria. Here is Aremu Ose:

AREMU OSE: Esi boda funwa
              Esi boda funwa
              Obasanjo Aremu, esi boda fun wa!
              Esi boda funwa

CHORUS: Esi boda funwa
                Esi boda funwa
                Obasanjo Aremu, esi boda fun wa!
                Esi boda funwa

AREMU OSE: Ajagun f'eyinti,
                Esi boda funwa!

CHORUS: Ajagun f'eyinti,
                Esi boda funwa

AREMU OSE: Olusegun Aremu
                Esi boda fun wa!

CHORUS: Olusegun Aremu
                Esi boda fun wa!

AREMU OSE: Olusegun Aremu
                Esi boda fun wa!

CHORUS: Olusegun Aremu
                Esi boda fun wa!

AREMU OSE: Olowu of Owu
                Esi boda fun wa!

CHORUS: Ajagun f'eyinti
                Esi boda fun wa!

AREMU OSE: Aisi boda yi o ma da
                Esi boda fun wa!
CHORUS: Ajagun f'eyinti
                Esi boda fun wa!
AREMU OSE: Aisi boda yi o ma da
                Esi boda fun wa!
CHORUS: Aisi boda yi o ma da
                Esi boda fun wa!
AREMU OSE: Open Border for us
                Open Border for us
                Obasanjo Aremu, open border for us
                Open border for us!
CHROUS: Open Border for us
                Open Border for us
                Obasanjo Aremu, open
AREMU OSE: Retired General
                OPEN BORDER FOR US

CHORUS:	Retired General
	Open border for us
AREMU OSE:	Olusegun Aremu
	Open border for us
CHORUS:	Olusegun Aremu
	Open border for us
AREMU OSE:	Olusegun Aremu
	Open border for us
CHORUS:	Olusegun Aremu
	Open border for us
AREMU OSE:	Olowu of Owu
	Open border for us
CHORUS:	Retired General
	Open border for us
AREMU OSE:	Not opening the border is bad enough
	Open border for us
CHROUS:	Not opening the border is bad enough
	Open border for us!

It is certain that Aremu Ose believes that the government's decision to close the Nigerian borders to importation of food is a very bad decision, since many Nigerians still don't get enough food to eat. He has, therefore, decided to use his poetry to address this topical issue and asks that the border be opened for the sake of the poor. It is a direct speech, "Open border for us!" as if it is an order by the traditional oral poet to the nation's president. The poet calls the president by different names, like a praise poetry, Obasanjo's praise name, Aremu (the poet and the president are obviously name sake), he calls him by his professional rank in the army, "General," and as far as I am concerned, it is like saying

> shame on you, General, you were to fight war to protect Nigeria, and now you cannot even fight to save our economy just by a simple understanding that you cannot close border if we do not have sufficient food to feed on.

The poet also addresses Obasanjo by his royal ancestry name, "Olowu of Owu," Obasanjo being from the Owu Royal House in Abeokuta. Just as this may be a persuasive strategy often used by oral poets to break down the wall of their patron and get what they requested, in my view the poet is probably also equating the role of a traditional ruler in Yoruba culture as protector of culture and traditional values and as one closer to the grassroots, the poet knows where it pinches his people. By invoking his royal ancestry name, the poet may be inferring that in contrast and despite his royal ancestry, the president has lost his bearing and no longer connects with the grassroots.[6] In any case, Aremu Ose champions the cause of the common man and takes his case to the seat of the civilian president of Nigerian: Open border for us/Not Opening the border is bad enough/Open border for us!

One very interesting area of this song is where the poet addresses issue of democracy in which every vote is a contract between the voter and the politician, and Aremu Ose is challenging the politician here that he has failed the contract, he has failed to do what the voters hired him to do:

AREMU OSE:	Gbogbo mekunu yanyan
	Alikawani taba Olusegun se
	Amuuse
	Asiika fun
	Aladigbo fun adigbo fun
	Osi wole
	Alkawani tie na
	Towa bawase
	Ki Obasanjo o MU SE
BOTO:	Alukawani si tobi ni waju Olohun!
EGBE:	Esi boda funwa
	Esi boda funwa
	Obasanjo Aremu, esi boda funwa!
	Esi boda funwa
AREMU OSE:	Aisi boda yi oma da
	Esi boda funwa!
EGBE:	Aisi boda yi oma da
	Esi boda funwa!
AREMU OSE:	Alukawani taa jose
	Kebi ma pa mekunu
	Ni gbogbo wa tife
EGBE:	Kebi ma pa mekunu
	Ni gbogbo wa ti fe
AREMU OSE:	Kiya maje mekunu
	Ni gbogbo wa ti fe
BOTO:	Olohun o ni f'ara niwa!
EGBE:	Kiya maje mekunu
	Ni gbogbo wa ti fe!

AREMU OSE:	Kara mani mekunu
	Ni gbogbo wa ti fe
EGBE:	Kara mani mekunu
	Ni gbogbo wa ti fe!
AREMU OSE:	Kara otu mekunu
	Ni gbogbo wa ti fe!
EGBE:	Kara out mekunu
	Ni gbogbo wa ti fe!
AREMU OSE:	All the downtrodden
	The promise we made to Obasanjo
	We fulfilled it
	We fulfilled it for him
	We said we would vote for him, we voted for him
	And he was elected
	His own promise
	Which he made to us
	Let Obasanjo fulfill it.
BOTO:	Promise is huge in the eyes of God!
CHORUS:	Open Border for us
	Open border for us
	Onasanjo Aremu, Open border for us
	Open border for us
AREMU OSE:	Not opening border is bad
	Open border for us
CHORUS:	Not opening border is bad
	Open border for us!
AREMU OSE:	The Promise we both made (Obasanjo and the people)
	The poor must not be hungry
	That's what we all want!
CHORUS:	The poor must not be hungry
	That's what we all want!
AREMU OSE:	The poor must not suffer
	That's what we all want!
BOTO:	God will not leave us in pains!
CHORUS:	The poor must not suffer
	That's what we all want!
AREMU OSE:	The poor must not be in pains
	That's what we all want!
CHORUS:	The poor must not be in pains
	That's what we all want!
AREMU OSE:	The poor must not be in pains
	That's what we all want!

*Alikawan*i, the poet here uses this word, *alikawani*, which can be translated as "the promise," but which actually is heavier than just a promise when used in Ilorin home of the poet, it means also the trust, the covenant, the deal, the agreement, in which you out of your free will entered into, or gave, what can be called, "your word, which is your honor," it has spirituality to it when used in Ilorin where there is a saying that, *Alikawani eru Olohun*, "Alikawani is the load of God," and the poet is, therefore, invoking this spirituality when he says the president must be accountable and fulfills the promise and the deal for which the voter voted for him to be president. The issue of campaign promise and accountability to the people is, therefore, given prominence. The repetition of "open border for us," "we fulfill our promise, fulfill yours," "the poor must not suffer," and "the poor must not be in pains" demonstrates the role of traditional oral poet as the mouthpiece of the ordinary people.

Yet, in another song, the economic well-being of the whole nation, Nigeria, takes a major concern of the poet. He has referred, as shown in some of the earlier songs we discussed in this chapter, to the need to farm and the need for politicians to honor their promises to the people regarding the welfare of the common man. Now, the economy of Nigeria, he is of the opinion that the government should pay closer attention to the value of the Nigerian currency. Here is how Aremu Ose puts it:

AREMU OSE:	Ebawa towo wa se o
	Ajagun f'ehinti ebawa towo wa se
	Olowu of Owu, Obasanjo ebawa towo wa se
	Bowo wa ti wa yi òdaa
	Ebawa towo wa se
	Bowo wa ti wa tele
	Laye Gowon
	Ni gbogbo wa tife
EGBE:	Bowo wa ti wa tele
	Laye Gowon
	Ni gbogbo wa tife
AREMU OSE:	B'owo maka ti wa tele
	Laye Gowon
	Nigbogbo wa tife
EGBE:	B'owo maka ti wa tele
	Laye Gowon
	Nigbogbo wa tife
AREMU OSE:	B'owo aropuleni ilu-ebo se wa tele
	Laye Gowon
	Nigbogbo wa tife

BOTO:	Kini kan o kamilaya bi eran tutu towa d'owon!
EGBE:	B'owo aropuleni ilu-ebo se wa tele
	Laye Gowon
	Nigbogbo wa tife
AREMU OSE:	Bi owo ilewe fasiti ti wa tele
	Laye Gown
	Nigbogbo wa tife
EGBE:	Bi owo ilewe fasiti ti wa tele
	Laye Gown
	Nigbogbo wa tife
AREMU OSE:	Bi owo edukesan ti wa tele
	Laye Gowon
	Nigbogbo wa tife
EGBE:	B'owo edukasan ti wa tele
	Laye Gowon
	Nigbogbo wa tife
AREMU OSE:	B'owo poli ti wa tele
	Laye Gowon
	Nigbogbo wa tife
EGBE:	B'owo poli ti wa tele
	Laye Gowon
	Nigbogbo wa tife
AREMU OSE:	B'owo ileiwe koleji se wa tele
	Laye Gown
	Nigbogbo wa tife
EGBE:	B'owo ileiwe koleji se wa tele
	Laye Gown
	Nigbogbo wa tife
AREMU OSE:	B'owo irinkole tiwa tele
	Laye Gowon
	Nigbogbo wa tife
EGBE:	B'owo irinkole tiwa tele
	Laye Gowon
	Nigbogbo wa tife[7]

AREMU OSE:	Repair the value of our currency
	Retired General, repair the value of our currency
	Olowu of Owu, Obasanjo, repair the value of our currency
	The current value of our currency is bad
	Repair the value of our currency
	The value of our currency
	During the reign of Gowon
	Is what we all want

CHORUS: The value of our currency
                  During the reign of Gowon
                  Is what we all want

AREMU OSE: The cost of (pilgrimage to) Maka
                  During the reign of Gowon
                  Is what we all want

CHORUS: The cost of (pilgrimage to) Maka
                  During the reign of Gowon
                  Is what we all want

AREMU OSE: The cost of flight to overseas
                  During the reign of Gowon
                  Is what we all want

BOTO: Nothing borders me like the cost of meat that has
                  skyrocketed!

CHORUS: The cost of flight to overseas
                  During the reign of Gowon
                  Is what we all want

AREMU OSE: The cost of University education
                  During the reign of Gowon
                  Is what we all want

CHORUS: The cost of University education
                  During the reign of Gowon
                  Is what we all want

AREMU OSE: The cost of NCE education
                  During the reign of Gowon
                  Is what we all want

CHORUS: The cost of NCE education
                  During the reign of Gowon
                  Is what we all want

AREMU OSE: The cost of polytechnic education
                  During the reign of Gowon
                  Is what we all want

CHORUS: The cost of polytechnic education
                  During the reign of Gowon
                  Is what we all want

AREMU OSE: The cost of post-primary education
                  During the reign of Gowon
                  Is what we all want

CHORUS: The cost of post-primary education
                  During the reign of Gowon
                  Is what we all want

AREMU OSE: The cost of iron sheet for building
                  During the reign of Gowon
                  Is what we all want

CHORUS: The cost of iron sheet for building
            During the reign of Gowon
            Is what we all want

The poet is passing a verdict on the government of Nigeria led by President Obasanjo that it has not been able to manage the economy well as the value of the Nigerian currency, and the cost of commodities has gone up beyond the reach of the common man. Aremu Ose mentions specific examples of activities and commodities important to people's growth and survival and how they have become ridiculously out of reach for the common man. Perhaps, even more interesting is the way the oral poet has compared the value of the Nigerian currency during Obasanjo's civilian presidency and the cost of commodities during a previous military regime led by Yakubu Gowon and expresses preference to what the value and costs used to be during the Gowon regime. Aremu Ose is pretty much saying Obasanjo's government should emulate whatever the Gowon government did to keep the value of our currency high and the cost of commodities low.

General Yakubu Gowon ruled from 1966 to 1975. It was during his regime that Nigeria fought a civil war between the federal government and the Biafra rebels led by Odumegwu Ojukwu. Gowon is seen as the hero of One Nigeria, having worked hard to ensure that the federal side won the war and also ensured the postwar reconciliation with a doctrine of "no losers no winners." It is on record that many Nigerians are very critical of Yakubu Gowon for not investing money in infrastructure and pursuing a good foresight for a stronger future Nigeria during his regime. In particular, many are critical that Gowon approved payment of what has come to be known as Odoji bonus to all Nigerian workers instead of using that money to build strong infrastructural and educational systems for Nigeria. It was said that Gowon had claimed that his problem was not money but how to spend it, which painted Nigeria as unable to determine its priorities for building a formidable country for its people. Obasanjo (who had been a military head of state himself from 1976 to 1979) served as a civilian president for eight years from 1999 to 2011. The oral poet is comparing the two regimes and feels that the currency was stronger during the Gowon regime and that people could satisfy their needs with smaller amount of money at that time compared to the economic difficulty during the second coming of Obasanjo as Nigerian leader. The poet does not give any respite to the Obasanjo government in this song. He also discusses later in the song, the issue of local production of commodities and feels that things produced locally such as petrol should not be more expensive for the use of ordinary persons in Nigeria. Here is how he presents this:

AREMU OSE: Irin ikole ni naijiriya
Se b'awa na latie ni nkan wa
Aa!
Nkan taani
Ose wale dowon gogo!

EGBE: Nkan taani
Ose wale dowon gogo!

AREMU OSE: B'owo simanti ti wa tele
Laye Gowon
Nigbogbo wa tife
Simanti, ni naijiriya
Se bawa na la ni nkanwa
Nkan taa ni,
Ose wale dowon gogo!

EGBE: Nkan taa ni,
Ose wale dowon gogo!

AREMU OSE: B'owo epo petiro ti wa tele
Laye Gowon
Nigbogbo wa tife
Epo petiro, ni naijiriya
E bawana latie ni nkanwa
Nkan ta ni
O se wale d'owon gogo!

EGBE: Nkan taa ni,
Ose wale d'owon gogo!

AREMU OSE: Obasanjo odowore o
O dowore o
O dowore Aremu
O dowore o!

EGBE: Obasanjo odowore o
O dowore o
O dowore Aremu
O dowore o!

AREMU OSE: Ajagun f'eyinti o dowore o
O dowore o
O dowore Aremu
O dowore o!

EGBE: Ajagun f'eyinti o dowore o
O dowore o
O dowore Aremu
O dowore o!

AREMU OSE:	Olowu of Owu
	Kabiyesi Oba alaye luwa
	O dowore o
	O dowore Aremu,
	O dowore o!
BOTO:	Allah o ran o lowo!
EGBE:	Ajagun f'eyinti o dowore o
	O dowore o
	O dowore Aremu,
	O dowore o!
AREMU OSE:	Oniwa se, won o ri se
	Eleyin nan se won o ri se
	Olusegun Aremu Obasanjo
	Eleketa lon se lo yi
	Aremu o dowore o
	O dowore o
	O dowore Aremu
	O dowore o!
BOTO:	Egbe dada, dada lope!
EGBE:	Aremu o dowore o
	O dowore Aremu
	O dowore o![8]

AREMU OSE:	Iron sheets for building in Nigeria
	Aren't we the producers of the commodity!
	Aa!
	What we produce locally
	Why would it be out of reach for us!
CHROUS:	What we produce locally
	Why would it be out of reach for us!
AREMU OSE:	The cost of cement
	During the reign of Gowon
	Is what we all want
	Cement in Nigeria
	Aren't we the producers of the commodity!
	What we produce locally
	Why would it be out of reach for us!
CHORUS:	What we produce locally
	Why would it be out of reach for us!
AREMU OSE:	The cost of petrol
	During the reign of Gowon

> Is what we all want
> Petrol in Nigeria
> Aren't we the producer of the commodity!
> What we produce locally
> Why should it be out of reach for us!

CHORUS: What we produce locally
> Why would it be out of reach for us!

AREMU OSE: Obasanjo, it's on your hands!
> It's on your hands
> It's on your hands, Aremu
> It's on your hands!

CHORUS: Obasanjo, it's on your hands!
> It's on your hands
> It's on your hands, Aremu
> It's on your hands!

AREMU OSE: Retired General, it's on your hands!
> It's on your hands
> It's on your hands, Aremu
> It's on your hands!

CHORUS: Retired General, it's on your hands!
> It's on your hands
> It's on your hands, Aremu
> It's on your hands!

AREMU OSE: Olowu of Owu
> Your Royal Highness, the King
> It's on your hands
> It's on your hands, Aremu
> It's on your hands!

BOTO: God will support you!

CHROUS: Retired General, it's on your hands!
> It's on your hands
> It's on your hands, Aremu
> It's on your hands!

AREMU OSE: The frontrunners tried it; they failed
> The back-runners tried it; they failed
> Olusegun Aremu Obasanjo
> You are spending your third term (in power)
> It's on your hands
> It's on your hands, Aremu
> It's on your hands!

BOTO: Chorus is well, a well-performed work is befitting!

CHORUS: Aremu, it's on your hands
> It's on your hands, Aremu
> It's on your hands!

The poet is demonstrating patriotism, in my view, by addressing the issue of local production and the cost of such commodity to the people of Nigeria. His insisting that the Government of Nigeria must look into the cost of locally produced goods, and that these goods must not be as expensive as imported materials, is quite interesting. What is, however, more interesting is the way the poet has invoked the right of the voters to take the elected officers into accountability. He said to the Nigerian president, "You are spending your third term (in power)/It's on your hands/It's on your hands, Aremu/It's on your hands!" In other words, Nigerians have given the president many opportunities to rule over them, and he must not fail them now and must do his best to reciprocate the good will of Nigerians! It is only a traditional African oral poet trained to do this kind of thing that does it at its best as Aremu Ose has done in this poetry!

Yes, the poet does not all the time address politics as topical issues. Sometime what is topical is the death of a popular community person, often a patron of the oral poet. It is common for the oral singer to seize on such opportunity to sing about this individual and about death and its destructive hands. The poet seizes on that to console the community and encourage the family of the deceased to take heart. The poet also takes this opportunity to teach morality, life philosophy, and cultural ethics about responsibility of human beings to the Almighty God and to humanity. One example, which is another popular song by Aremu Ose, is the song he sang for Duowoju Olooru, a socialite at Olooru in Moro Local Government Area of Kwara State. His death truly shook the community. Here is Aremu Ose:

AREMU OSE:	Durowoju
	Oba l'olooru
	Alamu Agbe wole
	O momo ku o
	Awuni tiwa tiwa
	Durowoju ku
	Alamu Agbe o mo dare
	Durowoju ku o
BOTO:	Olohun o yaafi ee
EGBE:	Duowoju uu
	Oba l'olooru u u u
	Alamu Agbe wole
	O momo ku o
	Awuni tiwa tiwa
	Durowoju ku

Alamu Agbe o mo dare
Durowoju ku o
AREMU OSE: Eja nla lo ninu omi
Durowoju lo l'olooru
Salami Alamu lo ni Moroo o
BOTO: Ile n lo nnkan mi

EGBE: Eja nla lo ninu omi ooo
Duowoju lo l'olooru u u u
Alamu Agbe lo ni Moroo oo
AREMU OSE: Ojo tin lo ilu Olooru
Ti mo ni ki won lo lee ke si direba mi fun mi
Ta a de bi ileewe nita wa
Ta a fe moo lo
Ni mo gbo ni kowee dun
Eye ko eye o wa
BOTO: Aya mi si ja pa a!
CHORUS: Eja nla lo ninu omi ooo
Duowoju lo l'olooru u u u
Alamu Agbe lo ni Moroo oo
AREMU OSE: Ngba ti mo de Ipata
Pe kin ki Jide Eleran
Ayoka 'mo Jimoh labe pa
Ni kowee tun dun
Eye ko eye o wa
BOTO: Mo fe sa pada lojo naa
CHORUS: Eja nla lo ninu omi ooo
Duowoju lo l'olooru u u u
Alamu Agbe lo ni Moroo oo
AREMU OSE: Mo tun de Maraba
Pe kin k'Alohunmata t'ilorin
Asomo doloriire
Isola ojo mole
Omo paramo to logbe
Isola omo Ajikobi
Oga ogun Mopa
Omo kusumu ba a ba d'Omoda
Ore e mi Isola tin sun oota fun moto
Ni kowee tun dun
Eye ko eye o wa!
BOTO: Oju mi doju ekun
EGBE: Eja nla lo ninu omi ooo
Duowoju lo l'olooru u u u
Alamu Agbe lo ni Moroo oo

AREMU OSE: Mo koja odo tin je Oyun
Nje ki nya sona Olooru
Ni kowee tun dun
Eye ko eye o wa!

BOTO: O ku maigida
Nle Sao

EGBE: Eja nla lo ninu omi ooo
Duowoju lo l'olooru u u u
Alamu Agbe lo ni Moroo oo

AREMU OSE: Nigba ti motun de Budo Sale
Gbogbo ara wa n fu mi
Eri mi wa n wu janin
Ni kowee tun dun
Eye ko eye o wa!

BOTO: Mo bas a pada leyin-in baba!

EGBE: Eja nla lo ninu omi ooo
Duowoju lo l'olooru u u u
Alamu Agbe lo ni Moroo oo

BOTO: Nle baa 'Bidun

AREMU OSE: Mo wa darin 'ja Olooru
Eeyan lo bilaa daadi
Bi egberun mejo
Mo ni ki la a de?
Won ni Salami omo Dare lo lo
Alamu Agbe tin be nle ta ate yii

BOTO: Ile n lo nnkan mii

EGBE: Eja nla lo ninu omi ooo
Duowoju lo l'olooru u u u
Alamu Agbe lo ni Moroo oo

AREMU OSE: Yo legbe yo legbe o
Popondo yo niso obi
Duowoju lo laarin ile Olooru
Alamu Agbe omo Momodu omo Dare
Omo Duowoju omo Dare
Alamu omo Momodu

BOTO: Olohun ma sa yaafi e

EGBE: Eja nla lo ninu omi ooo
Duowoju lo l'olooru u u u
Alamu Agbe lo ni Moroo oo[9]

AREMU OSE: Durowoju
King in Oloru
Alamu Agbe entered the ground

	He died indeed One admired deeply o his character Durowoju is dead Alamu Agbe child of Dare Durowoju died indeed!
BOTO:	May God forgive him!
CHORUS:	Durowoju King in Oloru One admired deeply o his character Durowoju is dead Alamu Agbe child of Dare Durowoju died indeed!
AREMU OSE:	The big fish has disappeared from water Durowoju has gone from Oloru Salami Alamu is gone from Moro
BOTO:	Ground swallows some substance
CHORUS:	Durowoju has gone from Oloru Salami Alamu is gone from Moro
AREMU OSE:	The day I was heading to Oloru And said I should enter my house to call my driver When we got to the school outside our compound And ready to go I heard the Kowe bird moaning The bird of Kowe the bird of Owa
BOTO:	And my chest beat in fear!
CHORUS:	The big fish has disappeared from water Durowoju has gone from Oloru Salami Alamu is gone from Moro
AREMU OSE:	When I got to Ipata I was going to greet Jide the meat seller Ayoka the child of Jimoh in Abepa Then the Kowe bird moaned again The bird of Kowe the bird of Owa!
BOTO:	I wanted to run back that day!
CHORUS:	The big fish has disappeared from water Durowoju has gone from Oloru Salami Alamu is gone from Moro
AREMU OSE:	I got to Maraba I wanted to greet Alohunmata of Ilorin He who makes one a lucky person Isola you resembles a Muslim The child of paramo that went to Ogbe

	Isola the child of Ajikobi
	The Lord of Ogun Mopa
	The Child of Kusumu when we get to Omoda
	My friend Isola who cried enough
	And the bird of Kowe moaned again
	The bird of Kowe the bird of Owa!
BOTO:	My eyes became crying eyes!
CHORUS:	The big fish has disappeared from water
	Durowoju has gone from Oloru
	Salami Alamu is gone from Moro
AREMU OSE:	I passed the River called Oyun
	Just about to branch to the road to Oloru
	The bird of Kowe moaned again
	The bird of Kowe the bird of Owa!
BOTO:	I greet you, owner of the house
	In the land of Sao!
CHORUS:	The big fish has disappeared from water
	Durowoju has gone from Oloru
	Salami Alamu is gone from Moro
AREMU OSE:	When I arrived Bode Saadu
	All my body now hinted me
	My head began to swell and expand
	And the Kowe bird moaned again
	The bird of Kowe the bird of Owa!
BOTO:	I ran away from the back of Baba!
CHORUS:	The big fish has disappeared from water
	Durowoju has gone from Oloru
	Salami Alamu is gone from Moro
BOTO:	Well done, the father of 'Bidun!
AREMU OSE:	I now arrived at the market square in Oloru
	People were beyond count
	Like eight thousand!
	I inquired what was the matter
	They said Salami the child of Dare was gone
	Alamu Agbe that is now under the ground that we walked on
BOTO:	The ground swallows some substance!
CHORUS:	The big fish has disappeared from water
	Duowoju has gone from Oloru
	Salami Alamu is gone from Moro
AREMU OSE:	He can carry it, he will be able to carry it
	Popondo descends from the market of kolanuts

Duowoju is gone from the town of Oloru
Alamu Agbe the child of Momodu the child of Dare
The child of Duowoju the child of Dare
Alamu the child of Momodu
BOTO: God please forgive him
CHORUS: The big fish has disappeared from water
Durowoju has gone from Oloru
Salami Alamu is gone from Moro

This song is obviously about a famous member of the community who has died, and it provided an opportunity for the oral poet to rally the community people around the issues of death, mortality, and tenderness of life and of human being. As a well-respected and honored person in the community, as a little "mighty" or "lord" in life, Duowoju, when he died, became that person buried under "the ground that we [all] walked on." The poet paints a picture of sorrow and calamity felt by the community people following the death of Duowoju, yet the inevitability of death makes them resigned to fate and accept their loss! Aremu Ose uses a storytelling method to celebrate Duowoju, invoking the "bird of bad news," the bird of tragedy, the bird of *Kowe* that appeared to him at every corner he went, announcing to him, through songs, "o dun," "it makes a hiss," gives signs or announces of the passing of Duowoju. "dun" the word that is used here, "Eye kowe dun," "Kowe bird sang," but "dun" is actually heavier than "singing" or "hissing." The bird wailed, it cried, it moaned, it howled, yet it sang, a kind of bitter way of singing! By invoking the Kowe bird, the bird of bad luck, the poet electrifies the air and creates the atmosphere for a perfect sense of mourning of the dead. This song for the dead is topical because it reflects an issue to which all community people are mobilized in sorrow at the period. Death itself is presented here as an enemy, a destroyer of happiness, a destroyer of joy, and creator of pain and sadness, and a snatcher of a person dearest to people! Duowoju is referred to as "the big fish" that has disappeared from water! This song also explores praise poetry by invoking the lineage of Duowoju: "Alamu Agbe the child of Momodu the child of Dare"! This song about death presents a great history of Duowojy's ancestry!

It is in performing topical songs such as presented in this chapter and in the force with which he sings them that Aremu Ose has been unique in Ilorin community. There are too many other examples that interested readers can explore in Ose's topical songs. He is a singer like no other one in the special skills that he uses. No discussion of Dàdàkúàdá in the twenty-first century can be complete without the discussion of this legend.

Notes

1 Aremu Ose, just like Odolaye Aremu, was always regarded as a competitor of Jaigbade Alao. Each had his own followers, and also there are fans that do not discriminate in their love for them.

2 Aremu Ose, "Alikurani Nsoro," Side 1, Record label, date unknown.

3 Ibid.

4 Ibid.

5 *Globalization, Oral Performance, and Traditional African Poetry* (2018): 73–82.

6 It must be noted that at this period, President Obasanjo has the public image of being very stubborn and hardly yielding. Aremu Ose is, therefore, putting up all efforts to "bend" him in favor of the need of ordinary Nigerians.

7 Aremu Ose, "Alikurani Nsoro," Side 2, Record label.

8 Ibid.

9 Aremu Ose, "Duowoju Olooru" Record label.

8 Aesthetic and didactic dimensions in Dàdàkúàdá

It has become a common process for me to explain to my American students in my African American folklore classes that the "anxiousness" of a traditional African audience of folk performances in seeing an "artistic perfection" does not translate to a sole preoccupation with a round character, a strong or poetic language, a well-constructed setting, or a lineal plot; it is not even of an overriding importance to them the ways these elements appear in a story! Artistic perfection of art in a traditional African perspective is an art that is for the sake of life of people and community even as the art contains humorous stories and uses onomatopoeic, repetition, and charming metaphors. The concern for community morality is overwhelming in the reasons for the performance of folktales, and the singers of oral songs are interested in how lineage trees are preserved and in what becomes of a child whose ancestry were warriors and defenders of community values. It was for this reason that I have repeatedly stated, therefore, that art, in the perspective of traditional Yoruba artists and their audiences, for example, is not an art for the sake of art but an art for the sake of life of the people and the community.

My discussion of aesthetic and didactic dimensions in Dàdàkúàdá in this chapter must be understood from this traditional Yoruba paradigm. The overpowering strength of the language used by the Dàdàkúàdá artist is not meant as an end in itself. The audience is constantly exploring to see what relevance the language has to the cultural and social reality of the community. How are the drummer's proverbs and the singer's performance techniques employed to advocate for society's progress while correcting its social upheavals? I will discuss the elements of Dàdàkúàdá aesthetics and didactic dimensions in this chapter by focusing on different areas of Dàdàkúàdá's songs and performances.

The use of language

The language of Dàdàkúàdá is completely in the Ilorin dialect of Yoruba, *Yoruba Ilorin.*[1] Some features that differentiate *Yoruba Ilorin* from other dialects of Yoruba include, for example, the use of vowel /O/: Oyo Yoruba will say *o n bo* (s/he's coming) and Ilorin Yoruba will say *in bo* (or what might sound in an Anglicized rendition as *orn bo*). Most of the places where /O/ is used in Oyo Yoruba, what sounds like an (or)—/ɔ/—is used in the *Yoruba Ilorin*. /O/ as in over, and (or)—/ɔ/ as in orange (or organ). It is in this way that the following example should be read. In Yoruba orthography, the /ɔ/ is represented by the inclusion of a diacritic [.] under [o] = [o̞]. *So o gbo ni?* (Oyo, "Don't you hear?"), *So.o. gbo. ni?* (Ilorin); *Ta lo n ba a wi* (Oyo, "To whom are you talking?"), *Ta lo. n baa wi* (Ilorin). In short, the language dialect of Dàdàkúàdá is completely the *Yoruba Ilorin* dialect. Other uses of language in Dàdàkúàdá are as found in all Yoruba oral poetry. The artists employ proverbs, images, metaphors, similes, lexical matchings, hyperbole, repetition, onomatopoeia, word play, and parallelism to make their message more vivid to the audience and to culturally enrich their poetry. It is often the case that each metaphor, parallelism, play-on-word, or proverb has anecdotes that are very deeply rooted in local meanings and cultural significance. We will isolate some Dàdàkúàdá songs and expressions for our discussion. Examples of some of the language uses are as follows:

1 Proverbs:

> Bi Sango ba n paraba, ti n ba n paroko bii tigi nla ko
> Oni Sango menni to le koju kiraju
> Ni so ju ina ki isu ewura o ma fii hu irun[2]

> If Sango kills Araba tree, kills Iroko tree, he dares not face the
>   monster tree
> The Sango worshiper knows whom he faces
> Not in the eye of fire will ewura yam grow hair.

> Abere alase ohun ase ni
> Owu alase, ohun ase ni
> Alao ni bi to nlo, a ware ni.[3]

> The needle of a magician, is always with magic
> The thread of magician, is always with magic
> Alao wherever you go, we are always with you.

Bo pe ile a mo
Bo pe ile a mo
Elee kisa tí njo loru, bope-ile a mo.[4]

However lengthy it is, the day will break
However lengthy it is, the day will break
The man in rags who dances in the cover of night, the day
   will break.

However powerful these proverbs are, it is clear from close consideration that they are rooted in history, culture, metaphysics, and spirituality. All these meanings are not lost to the audience even as they
enjoy the abstract attraction of the language use in these songs. Our
second example is very interesting for many reasons. The items of reference are *abere* (needle), *owu* (thread), and *ase* (magic) (or it might
actually be *ate*, the hawking tray); these are all common elements that
make their use show how rooted the singers and the songs are to the
grassroots. I am not sure the English translations of these cultural
words are adequate (e.g., the meaning of *ase* is certainly not what a
common Westerner understands as magic)!

2 Images:

Aaa, bayi lapasa n hun soo
Ase bayi Latojere nse wahala o to meja wale
N o tete mo, n o tete mo,
Aaa, bayi lero eyin odi nse wahala ki won o to mowo wale.[5]

Aaa, this is the way the loom produces the cloth
So, this is the way Latojere suffers before he brings fish home
I didn't realize, I didn't realize,
Aaa, that this is the way people who go trading suffer before
   they bring money home.

Again, images of struggle, suffering, courage, and commitment are
painted in the song. The idea of "No pain and No gain" is fundamental to the ways the anecdotes in this song are presented: the loom
works hard, the fishermen struggles, and the trader does not rest, and
all their efforts lead to successes in their various endeavors. The use of
these images definitely is intended to show that every pain sustained in
the process of righteousness would lead to gains. The loom, the fisher-
man, and the trader are all hard workers, and all have reasons to smile,
even the loom that is an object, because it is credited with success!

Another image here is that of know-how, or skills, or expertise, without which each of the items would not succeed.

3   Metaphors:

>   Oni kopi lasan, ko maa so pe orin awa kere si tohun
>   Ki oromadie komo so pe asa nla gba ngba kere so hun
>   Eye tintin, komo so pe eye Ogongo kere sohun,
>   Oo rayi mawa ara![6]

>   Mere plagiarist, to be saying that our songs are inferior to his
>   For chicken to be saying that the mighty hawk is inferior to him
>   For tit bird to be saying that the ostrich is inferior to him,
>   can't you see self-inflation!

The metaphors used are self-explanatory. The poet creates a case for juxtaposition, for irony, and for comparison: chicken versus the mighty hawk, tit bird versus the ostrich, inferior versus superior! It is a song of thesis and antithesis, and the mere metaphorical juxtapositions in the above song make it attractive to the ear! Each of the remaining samples present clear meanings of their cultural and artistic contents. Simile, hyperbole, lexical matching, word play, and repetition, each serves a purpose of artistic and cultural strengths for the poetry. In some cases, the use of repetition, cultural emphasis, and artistic beauty are displayed.

4   Simile:

>   Too ba de Ita aburo ti Ilorin
>   E lo wo masalasi Alao gbede to ko
>   Ee se bi e de Madina ni.[7]

>   When you arrive at Aburo area in Ilorin
>   Go and see the Mosque built by Alao gbede
>   You will think yau have arrived at Madina.

5   Hyperbole:

>   Yaarasula llahi!
>   Eni to ba kirun nibi Masalasi taa wi yi,
>   Nita aburo, Masalasi Alao gbede,
>   Ina Olohun dee wo fun.[8]

>   Oh the messenger of God!
>   Whoever prays in this mosque we're talking about

In Aburo area, the mosque of Alao gbede,
The hell of God is forbidden for him.

Ko si bi to lohun o si
A ma Ilorin ni n sun.[9]

There is no place where God is not present
But He sleeps in Ilorin.

Adisa, n o pe o laye
Won o si gbo lorun.[10]

Adisa, I shall praise you in this world
And they will hear in heaven.

6   Lexical matching:

Ba a ba ranti Bello to ku
O ye kaki Bello to ku.[11]

If we remember Bello that dies
We ought to praise Bello that remains.

7   Word play (or word creation)

Woriwo riwowo
Dikan gbari gaja, *gbogbo ara kan go o.*[12]
Gbari n gbasa!

Woriwo riwowo (no meaning, simply exclamation)
Dikan gbari gaja, all the body aches
Gbari n gbasa! (a heavy exclamatory sound, indication of a
    torturous pain)

8   Repetition:

LEADER:	Oya mo de
CHORUS:	O ya mo de
LEADER:	Eku ale
CHORUS:	Eku ale
LEADER:	Eku ale o
CHORUS:	Eku ale o
LEADER:	Mo gbere mi de
CHORUS:	Mo gbere mi de.[13]
LEADER:	Now, I have come

CHORUS:	Now, I have come
LEADER:	Good evening
CHORUS:	Good evening
LEADER:	Good evening
CHORUS:	Good evening
LEADER:	I'm here with my play (songs)
CHORUS:	I'm here with my play.

Repetition is one of the most popular features of oral poetry, and in the above poem, it shows that repetition is a purposeful cultural and artistic element for the oral singer or in many cases for a folktale narrator. The Yoruba people have an adage that if someone keeps repeating something, if that thing is not painful to him, then it must be soothing for him.

Political discourse in Dàdàkúàdá

As we have seen in the last chapter, the Dàdàkúàdá poets sing political songs. Odolaye Aremu remained the most partisan of all the Dàdàkúàdá poets. The last chapter shows that he was the poet to many politicians in Yoruba land. He sang for both regional and national politicians, and perhaps even carried political party membership. At least, he publicly declared membership in political party even if he does not carry their membership cards. Although I was unable to confirm this directly from him, I strongly believe that his declaration of party partisanship in his songs may be strong evidence to believe that he was indeed a card-carrying member of different political parties throughout the Nigerian republic up to his death. As we already discussed, he was known in many circles to be a poet of Akintola, the former Premier of Nigerian Western Region. He also sang for Shehu Shagari, the second republic president of Nigeria. He sang for Adedibu, the strongman of Ibadan politics. Locally, in Ilorin, he followed and sang for Abubakar Olusola Saraki, the Ilorin-Asa-Moro constituency National Senator and former Senate Leader. The last chapter tried to do some justice to Odolaye and his politics and partisanship. Yet, some of his political songs will be re-quoted and rediscussed here as evidences of strong political commitment of Dàdàkúàdá artists. However, since his death in 1997, it seems that Aremu Ose, another Ilorin Dàdàkúàdá poet whose poetry does not shy away from heavy dose of political touch, briefly took over as the highly partisan of the twenty-first-century Dàdàkúàdá artists. His partisanship songs definitely show his public support for national and local political leaders, and in particular, they also show which contemporary political leadership he was ready to publicly campaign against. He was a rarely brave poet who sang against a sitting governor of a state in representing the voice and yearnings of his Ilorin people. He called the governor a thug and advocated that his end was imminent! He said the governor would be thrown to the dustbin of history. Our first set of examples would come from Odolaye's poetry, followed by Aremu Ose's.

1   Aye fele fele, Aiye fee le lu kan raa won
    Iya si nje omo elomii bii ko jade laye
    Ama awon Olosi eyan, kara nbani eyan, omo ale eyan,
    Won se b'olohun go ni,
    Oba tii dani tan tii duro ti ni
    Allanu Rabbi tii duro tini nigba eru ba fe wo.[14]

    The world is very light, almost torn apart
    Some people suffer as if they should quit the world
    But some stupid people, useless people, idiot people,
    They think God is senseless,
    Allahu Rabbi (My God) who stays with one when his burden is
    getting unbearable!

This particular song is rather very philosophical but yet political. Society has changed in such ways that leaders now don't really care about their followers, and the ordinary people who hitherto could count on their leaders' help, are now abandoned to suffer untold hardships. What is also unique about this song is the kind of anger that the poet displays while addressing those he says think God is senseless. He describes them as "stupid, useless and idiot people"! Those who know Odolaye well would explain that abusive words are characteristic of his poetic outbursts and often contribute to his use of hyperbolism. As I have discussed before, Odolaye is a major referent whenever Ilorin traditional oral singer is described as *eleke eebu*, one with a mouthful of insults! I pointed out that Odolaye in a song calls himself Aja Kwara, the Dog of Kwara State! The metaphor of a dog here is that which pursues a thief or chases a prey in the forest. In that song, Odolaye says his dog does not bark for no cause: it barks because it sees an animal prey or a human daemon! This name almost became his nickname before he died. I have heard people called him, *Aja kwara ti e gbo lasan*, the Kwara dog that doesn't bark for no cause! The idea of a traditional African poet as a dog is quite effective indeed, especially in the postcolonial crisis that engulfs Africa, where politicians are deeply corrupt and where traditional institutions have compromised on ethics, morality, and community values.

2   On the division of Ibadan people on political linings in the second republic:

Okunrin Ibadan, Obirin Ibadan
Kekere Ibadan, Agba Ibadan
Mo so funyin, E pe ra yinjo eba rayin soro
Epa manran po ki gbogbo kini ohun o jo 'kan
Naijiriya yi Olohun oni jo o daru ma lae lae.[15]

Men of Ibadan, women of Ibadan
Younger ones of Ibadan, elder ones of Ibadan
I have told you, you should come together
And talk (truth) to yourselves
Be united in decisions so that everything will be one.
This Nigeria, God will not allow confusion again.

3   On Obasanjo, as Nigeria's former Head of State:

Agbadun Obasanjo pupo
Obasajo, ooko isoman nii man omo laa
Agbadun Obasanjo,
Ee ri gbogbo Naijiriya ti toro ti gbogbo re ndun yin
O ni laakayi pupo, o lopolo pupo
Ko fi gba kan bo kan ninu.[16]

We enjoyed Obasajo very well
Obasanjo, the name given to a child is what fits the child
We enjoyed Obasanjo
Can't you see that the whole of Nigeria is peaceful and very sweet
He is very bright, he is very brilliant
He does not but one calabash into the other.

The Obasanjo song was clearly a commendation of his decision to hand over power to an elected democratic government in Nigeria in 1979. The poet infers, as the Yorubas often do, that persons would live up to the meanings of the names given to them by their parents. "Obasanjo" in Yoruba means "God has repaid the good person(s)"—such a name can be given to a newly born child by her/his parents to signify that the birth of the baby was a reward to them by God. The name might also be given to a baby to indicate that something might have recently happened in the lives of the parents. The implication here is that the people had done some good in their lives and might have faced difficulty in accomplishing the good deed, and now, God is rewarding them as a sign that He has not forgotten the hardship they faced carrying out the good deed. Yet, the meanings of *Obasanjo* might also include the fact that the baby would grow to be a person of God, or one who would be close to or favorable to God, being a good person himself or herself. The poet here shows this as an evident that Obasanjo was a good person who was doing what was good for Nigeria.

4   Here, Odolaye Aremu is provoking Shagari, the first Executive President of Nigeria:

To, ta lo lohun o gba ti e
Naijiriya toni,
Igba taa bi taani tan, labi taa ni!
O o ma je won o fowo lale le o lowo man
Gbogbo awon Agbaagba Naijiriya,
Won wa leyin re o,
Ma so jo, I ran babare o gbodo sojo.[17]

Now, who says he's not for you
In Nigeria of today!
After given birth to whom, was whom!
Better don't allow them to dictate to you again.
All the elders of Nigeria are behind you.
Don't fear, descedents of your father must not fear.

5   On the political wrangling among Adamu Atta, then governor of Kwara State, Mahmud Akanbi Oniyangi, then Nigerian Minister of Defense, Sulu Gambari, then Emir of Ilorin, and Abubakar Olusola Saraki, the poet sings:

A man edakun, e ro wo!
Bi erin meji ba n ja ni nu igbo,
Aaaa, koko, eruwa, gbogbo igi inu igbe oo
Lara o man ta a
Eyin eyan jankan-jankan,
Dokita Saraki, Sulu Gambari, Akanbi Oniyangi, Adamu Atta,
Kilo se tee le perayin jo,
Ke barayin soro,
Ki gbogbo Kwara o toro,
Ka ma rije, ka ma ri mu, ka ma rale, kamaa kole
Ki oni kaluku o maa tun aye Babare se.[18]

But please, have a thought!
When two elephants fight in the forest,
Aaaa, grasses, every tree in the bush
Shall have pain on their body
All you big, big people,
Doctor Saraki, Sulu Gambari, Akanbi Oniyangi, Adam Atta,
Why can't you call yourselves together
And talk (truth) to yourselves,
So that the whole Kwara State can be peaceful,
So that we can have (enough) to eat, to drink, to buy land, to
    build houses
So that everyone can develop his father's place.

I have discussed these songs in the previous chapter. However, they show clearly how much this oral singer has involved himself and dedicated his songs to community's political issues. Let us now see some examples from Aremu Ose, who, like Odolaye, reflected on political happenings at the local and national scenes in Nigeria. On the skyrocketing prices of goods in Nigeria around 2005, Ose blamed the Obasanjo government for a policy of restricting importations of food and other amenities. He sings:

OSE: Olusegun Aremu
    Esi boda fun wa!

CHORUS: Olusegun Aremu
    Esi boda fun wa!

OSE: Olowu of Owu
    Esi boda fun wa!

CHORUS: Ajagun f'eyinti
    Esi boda fun wa!

OSE: Aisi boda yi o ma da
    Esi boda fun wa!

CHORUS: Ajagun f'eyinti
    Esi boda fun wa!

OSE: Aisi boda yi o ma da
    Esi boda fun wa!
CHORUS: Aisi boda yi o ma da
    Esi boda fun wa!
OSE: Gbogbo mekunu yanyan
    Alikawani tab a Olusegun se

Amuuse
Asiika fun
Aladigbo fun adigbo fun
Osi wole
Alkawani tie na
Towa bawase
Ki Obasanjo o mu se

BOTO: Alukawani sit obi ni waju Olohun!

CHORUS: Esi boda funwa
Esi boda funwa
Obasanjo Aremu, esi boda fun wa!
Esi boda funwa

OSE: Aisi boda yi o ma da
Esi boda fun wa!

CHORUS: Aisi boda yi o ma da
Esi boda fun wa!

OSE: Olusegun Aemu
Open the border for us

CHORUS: Olusegun Aemu
Open the border for us

OSE: Olowu of Owu
Open the border for us!

CHORUS: Olowu of Owu
Open the border for us!

OSE: Retired Military Officer
Open the border for us!

CHORUS: Retired Military Officer
Open the border for us!

OSE: Leaving the border closed is wickedness
Open the border for us!

CHORUS: Leaving the border closed is wickedness
Open the boder for us!

OSE: All poor, downtrodden people
Our promise to Olusegun
We have stood by our promise

We have fulfilled our promise to him
We said we would vote for him and we voted for
 Him
And he was re-elected President
His own promise
The one he made with us
Obasanjo must fulfill it!

BOTO: A Promise is huge before the Almighty God!

CHORUS: Open the border for us
 Open the border for us
 Obasanjo Aremu, Open the border for us
 Open the border for us!

Opening borders between Nigeria and its neighboring countries are now seen as crucial for an uplift of life for ordinary Nigerian. In the global century where transnational migration and movement of people across the world becomes a choicest pursuit of economic well-being and personal comfort especially by people from less-developed countries, it might be easy to think the oral singer is making a case for freedom to migrate internationally for the downtrodden. Aremu Ose is actually here not referring to people but to goods: importation of food and other essential goods into Nigeria. I think the poet's wisdom is that if food, which is cheap and plenty in one nation, is easily imported and distributed widely across another country, people across the world would have less cause to migrate to other countries. I believe his reason is strengthened by a Yoruba adage that says *Bi ebi ba ti tan ninu ise, is buse*, meaning "Once hunger is eliminated from poverty, then poverty is ended!" Yet, we can see that in this song, the singer makes a case for responsible politics where voters and elected officers enter into conveyance and each fulfilling their promise. In other words, once politicians get elected into office, they must be held responsible for the promise they made to the electorates. Aremu Ose is telling the Nigeria President Olusegun Obasanjo publicly that he got into office as president on the back of poor Nigerians who voted for him, and that it was his turn to fulfill the promise he made to Nigerians! The fulfillment of one promise must lead to fulfillment of the other! In the twenty-first-century Africa, Ose's responsible politics must be central to the concept of good governance being championed by African political leadership through their NEPAD project.

 Yet, while continuing the performance, Ose went into some of the other crises faced by Nigeria and many other poor nations of the world in the global century; in particular, the crisis of weak currency in the face of the mighty strong currencies of the industrialized nations. He also addressed the problem of the goods that are extremely expensive and outside the purchasing power of ordinary people. In this song, Ose recognized the fact that Nigeria was an agrarian nation but queried why even those products that Nigeria produced are outside the rich of common people! Here is Ose and his performance group:

OSE: Obasanjo,
      Ebawa towo wa se o,
      Ajagun f'eyinti ebawa towo wa se
      Olowu of Owu, Obasanjo ebawa towo wa se
      Bowo wa ti wa yi òdaa
      Ebawa to'wo wa se
      Bowo wa ti wa tele
      Laye Gowon
      Nigbogbo wa tife

CHORUS: Bowo wa ti wa tele
      Laye Gowon
      Nigbogbo wa tife

OSE: B'owo maka ti wa tele
      Laye Gowon
      Nigbogbo wa tife

CHORUS: B'owo maka ti wa tele
      Laye Gowon
      Nigbogbo wa tife

OSE: B'owo aropulani ilu-ebo se wa tele
      Laye Gowon
      Nigbogbo wa ti fe

BOTO: Kini kan o kamilaya bi eja tutu towa d'owon!

CHORUS: B'owo aropulani ilu-ebo se wa tele
      Laye Gowon
      Nigbogbo wa ti fe

OSE: Bi owo ilewe *fasiti* ti wa tele
      Laye Gowon
      Ni gbogbo wa ti fe

CHORUS: B'owo *fasiti* ti wa tele
Laye Gowon
Ni gbogbo wa ti fe

OSE: Bi owo ilewe *edukesan* ti wa tele
Laye Gowon
Ni gbogbo wa ti fe

OSE: B'owo *edukesan* ti wa tele
Laye Gowon
Ni gbogbo wa ti fe

OSE: B'owo ilewe *poli* ti wa tele
Laye Gowon
Ni gbogbo wa ti fe

OSE: B'owo *poli* ti wa tele
Laye Gowon
Ni gbogbo wa ti fe

OSE: B'owo ileiwe *Koleji* se wa tele
Laye Gowon
Ni gbogbo wa ti fe

CHORUS: B'owo *Kolej*i se wa tele
Laye Gowon
Ni gbogbo wa ti fe

OSE: B'owo irin ikole ti wa tele
Laye Gowon
Ni gbogbo wa ti fe

CHORUS: B'owo irinikoole ti wa tele
Laye Gowon
Ni gbogbo wa ti fe

OSE: Irin ikole ni naijiriya
Se b'awa na latie ni nkan wa
Aa!
Nkan taani
Ose wale dowon gogo!

CHORUS: Nkan taani
Ose wale dowon gogo!

OSE: B'owo simanti ti wa tele
Laye Gowon

Ni gbogbo wa ti fe
Simanti, ni naijeiya
Se bawa na la ni nkanwa
Nkan taa ni,
Ose wale d'owon gogo!

CHORUS: Nkan taani
O se wale dowon gogo!

OSE: B'owo epo petiro ti wa tele
Laye Gowon
Nigbogbo wa ti fe
Epo petiro, ni naijiriya
E bawana latie ni nkan wa
Nkan ta ni
O se wale d'owon gogo!

CHORUS: Nkan taani
Ose wale dowon gogo!

OSE: Obasanjo
You must work to strengthen our currency
Retired Soldier (Obasanjo), you must work to strengthen our
    currency
Olowu of Owu, you must work to strengthen our currency
The current weakness of our currency is not good
You should strenthen our currency
Exactly how our currency was
During the Gowon era,
Is what we all want!

CHROUS: Exactly how our currency was
During the Gowon era,
Is what we all want!

OSE: How the fare to Macca was
During the Gowon era
Is what we want

CHROUS: Exactly how our currency was
During the Gowon era,
Is what we all want!

OSE: How plane fare to Europe was
During the Gowon era
Is what we want

BOTO: Nothing makes me sad like the price of fresh fish that has gone beyond (our) purchansing power!

CHROUS: Exactly how plane fare to Europe was
During the Gowon era
Is what we want

OSE: How university tuitin was
During the Gowon era
Is what we want

CHORUS: How university tuitin was
During the Gowon era
Is what we want

OSE: How College of Education tuition was
During the Gowon era
Is what we want

CHORUS: How College of Education tuition was
During the Gowon era
Is what we want

OSE: How Polytechnique tuition was
During the Gowon era
Is what we want

CHROUS: How Polytechnique tuition was
During the Gowon era
Is what we want

OSE: How high school tuition was
During the Gowon era
Is what we want

CHORUS: How high school tuition was
During the Gowon era
Is what we want

OSE: How the cost of building materials (iron) was
During the Gowon era
Is what we want

CHORUS: How the cost of building materials (iron) was
During the Gowon era
Is what we want

OSE: Building materials (iron) in Nigeria
Aren't we the makers and owners of them!

Why?
What belong to us
Why should it be out of our reach!

CHORUS: What belong to us
Why should it be out of our reach!

OSE: How the cost of cement was before
During the Gowon era
Is what we all want
Cement in Nigeria
Arent we the owners of it!
What belong to us
Why should it be out of our reach!

CHORUS: What belong to us
Why should it be out of our reach!

OSE: How the cost of petroleum was before
During the Gowon era
Is what we want
Petroleum in Nigeria
Aren't we the owners of it!
What belong to us
Why should it be out of our reach!

CHORUS: What belong to us
Why should it be out of our reach!

The above songs are examples of how Dàdàkúàdá poets address contemporary politics of our day and represent the ordinary person in their critical political discourse. Their political songs include what can be described as the songs about bread and butter, and here they are vehement in championing the cause of the downtrodden in the society.

Moral touch and other didactic functions of Dàdàkúàdá

The examples of moral and other didactic songs we will use here are how Dàdàkúàdá addresses each person's responsibility to the other, as being one's brother or sister's keeper. This is the ultimate morality in the society, which the poet is out to protect. Mostly, the poets advise the people and instruct them on good neighborliness. They also talk about family matters and call for unity. They tell people to march gently on the land. Even the land should deserve respect. Moreover, to walk gently is not to be over one's head. It is also to recognize the need for humility and personal limitations however physically strong or materially wealthy one may be. Oftentimes, the Dàdàkúàdá singer claims that his song is a *nasia*, or *isiti*, that is, a moral warning, or a reminder to the general populace!

E ba je ka parada lati serere
Eni to ba serere laye
Oluware lo leeso rere lorun
Eni to ba wuwa to le pupo
Ohun o wa ni duro jaye
Bo ba si pe laye,
Bo ba dorun koni ba nkan dada.[19]

You should let us change for (doing) good actions
He who does good in the world
Would reep good fruits in the heaven
He who displays very bad character
Would not wait to enjoy the world
And if he lives long in the world,
When he gets to heaven, he will not meet anything decent.

Nkan merin n bo waye, merin o te le
Igba ti aye o ba ni laari ma, merin o pada seyin
Owo n bo wale aye, Iyi o te le,
Ngba ti aye oni laari ma, Iyi pada seyin
Ogun n bo wale aye, kasaa koje te le
Ngba ti aye oni lari ma, kasa koje pada o wa kogun
Oba n bo wale aye, ase pelu iko lo te le,
Ngba ti aye oni lari ma, ase pada osi koba.
Eri bati bo tan aye ti nri,
Won wa ni biri lo ko n da, biri laye n yi,
Moniro le pa, a ye o yi bo bi kan kan
Nbi ojo ti n yo niti nyo, nibi orun ti nwo ni ti n wo,
Ile-aye o yi bo bi kankan, awon eyan ti n be n be ni npawada.[20]

Four things are coming to the world, and four things shall follow
    them
When the world becomes useless, four things shall go back
Money is coming to the world, honor shall follow
When the world becomes useless, honor goes back
Juju (or Native medicine) is coming to the world, workability
    follows
When the world becomes useless, the workability goes back and
    remains the

Medicine/juju
The king is coming to the world, royalty and authority follow
When the world becomes useless, authority goes back, remains
    the king
Can't you see how the world is becoming!
They say it is the vehicle that turns fast, the world that turns fast
I say they tell a lie, the world turns nowhere
The day rises where it does, and the sun sets where it does,
The world turns nowhere, it's the people occupant (of the world)
    that changes behavior.

Dokita Saraki,
Bo ba ko too ba ku
Ota odun mehindilogun, won o do re re o.[21]

Doctor Saraki
If you refuse to die (or if you live long enough)
The enemy of fiteen years standing, they will become your friend.

Almost every one of these didactic songs has important philosophical connotations. It goes without saying that morality in traditional Africa is defined from basic humanistic values, and moral metaphors are derived from what the society sees as natural environmental and humanistic truths. Imagine the powerful line, "The day rises where it does, and the sun sets where it does!" And indeed it is true! I don't think anyone would insist that the direction of sunrise and sunset have changed since his or her birth. One can say, for example, that the world has remained its beautiful and resourceful entity, and the crisis of global warming and troubles of harsh weather that we face in the twenty-first century are as a result of changes in human behavior and reflections of human wickedness on the environment.

The influence of Hausa on the language of Dàdàkúàdá poetry

Hausa has a number of influences on Dàdàkúàdá. This includes the use of Hausa language and proverbs in Dàdàkúàdá poetry. This reality can be easily traced to the multilingual and multicultural setting of Ilorin. The Ilorin people of different ethnic backgrounds have interacted over the ages and the Ilorin Yoruba reflects the multiethnicity of its abode. More than this, however, Hausa and Fulani languages generally enjoy a higher status in Ilorin for the simple reason that Ilorin's King is an ethnic Fulani and many of the Ilorin Fulanis have Hausa cultural linkages. These are examples of some songs with Hausa language extensions:

Aaji Shehu Shagari, asauka lafiya asauka lafiya
Allah ya bada sa'a
Allah ya bada samun alheri
Allah ya baka dogon rai.[22]

Alhaji Shehu Shangari, may you complete (your tenour) well
May Allah give you success
May Allah let you reep blessings
May Allah give you long life.

Ruwan zafi maganin kwadeyi
Aljunfun baya, mai wasta hannu
Asoroo kowobo bi apo eyin
Apo taa da leyin won o se fowo si rara
Gege b'Hausa ti n wi.[23]

Hot water, medicine for avaricious eater
Back pocket, spreads the hand
He who is difficult to insert hand in, like the back pocket
The pockets sewed to the back are difficult to put hands in,
Like the Hausas say.

Conclusion

We can see from the analysis in this chapter that aspects of Parry/
Lord theories on the composition and delivery of oral poetry which
Dandatti Abdul Kadir discusses as true for Shata Katsina's waka may
also be true of Dàdàkúàdá.[24] Yet, the Dàdàkúàdá poets, just like any
African oral singer, are very creative and make occasional improvements on the pattern, style, and techniques of delivery. This can be
seen in the trends in the different stages of Dàdàkúàdá development.
The general characteristic features of Yoruba oral poetry identified by
Olaitan, Babalola, and Olaosebikan are very true of Dàdàkúàdá poetry.[25] Finnegan's contention[26] that performance and composition are
separate in oral poetry is not particularly true of Dàdàkúàdá poetry.
It is absolutely postcolonial for oral artists to compose before they go
to recording studios to produce records. Even then, their initial compositions and what they subsequently deliver in the record houses are
not totally the same, perhaps not even 50% similar when one considers
all aspects of oral performance that go into making the record! Even
after they have practiced and specified the songs they would perform

for a particular record, it is the moment of performance that dictates how they say and sing a song. Their initial rehearsals in preparation for recording studios are more helpful with the theme of the songs, who to praise, and probably who to praise first, second, and so on. Yet, many Dàdàkúàdá poets do not do these modern-day prerecording rehearsals at all.[27] In my May 2008 interview with Jaigbade Alao, he confirmed that the only time his group rehearsed was when he was preparing for a new record. Yet, as a poet who began as a professional poet completely unable to read and write in the Yoruba language, Jaigbade, as I suspect a few other Dàdàkúàdá poets, now is able to write and read and indicated to me that he actually also does use writing in preparing for new records as well. Since he as leader is in control of the themes and songs chosen, and prepared for the new records, he would write them out ahead of the actual appearance at the recording studio. Yet, it must be reemphasized that nothing I have seen in contemporary performance of oral poetry show that the influence of prior performance practice and writing go beyond helping to arrange themes, identify songs, and support the actual practice of those songs. Whereas field performance is almost a daily affair, records are turned out only occasionally and at most a typical Dàdàkúàdá group produces one or two records in a year. It takes leading Dàdàkúàdá artists like Jaigbade to do more than two records in any one year! This fact shows the limitations of prior practice and writing in the life of Dàdàkúàdá performances!

Finally, like all oral poetry, Dàdàkúàdá's beauty lies, among other areas, in its different techniques of performance and its use of language. I expect that our discussions in this chapter will serve as a foundation for future works on different aspects of Dàdàkúàdá poetry and on individual Dàdàkúàdá poets.

Notes

1 Many people wrongly classify it as *Yoruba Oyo* (i.e. Oyo dialect of Yoruba). Olajubu also does the same in the footnote on page 2 of his M.A. Thesis on "Iwi: Egungun Chants in Yoruba Oral Literature," of the U of Lagos (1970).

2 Aremu Ose, "Yerepe gbarare gbagi oko," Shanu Olu Records LP SOS 136 A, 1981.

3 Jaigbade Alao, "Kole bawa logigi," Chief Records LP CRL 001 E, 1987.

4 Jaigbade Alao, "Kole bawa logigi," Chief Records LP CRL 001 E, 1987. Also from his field performance in Ode Igbonna, Edun, Ilorin, on 30 December 1987.

5 Odolaye Aremu, "E Saalo Faye," Olatunbosun Records ORCLP 151 A, 1982.

6 Aremu Ose, "Yerepe gbarare gbagi oko," Shanu Olu Records LP SOS 136 A, 1981.
7 Odolaye Aremu, "Sheku Shagari Geri Ijoba," Amiyo Sound A SSLP 058A, 1979.
8 Ibid.
9 Odolaye Aremu, "Elenini Aye," Ariyo Sound ASSLP 058B, 1979.
10 Jaigbade Alao, "Ko lebawa logigi," Chief Records LP CRL CO1E, 1987.
11 Odolaye Aremu, "Elenini Aye," Ariyo Sound ASSLP 058B, 1979.
12 Aremu Ose, "Yerepe gbarare gbagi oko," Shemu Olu LP SOS 136A 1981. From the whole lines, only the underlined is meaningful.
13 Some lines from the field performance of Jaigbade Alao on 30 December 1987. Ile Igbonna, Ilorin.
14 Odolaye Aremu, "E saalo Faye," Olatunbosun Records ORCLP 151A, 1982.
15 Odolaye Aremu, "Sheku Shagari Geri Ijoba," Ariyo Sound ASSLP 058E, 1979.
16 Ibid.
17 Odolaye Aremu, "Shehu Shangari Geri Ijoba," Ariyo Sound ASSLP 058A, 1979.
18 Ibid., "Elsalo faye," Olatunbosun Records ORCLP 151A, 1982.
19 Jaigbade Alao, "Kole Bawa Logigi Ma," Chief Records LP CRL 001E, 1987.
20 Personal interview with Jaigbade Alao, 9 August 1987. He chants the lines on the interview.
21 Odolaye Aremu "E Saalo Faye," Olatunbosun Records ORCLP 151A, 1982. Labanji Bolaji, in his article, "Obasanjo versus E Ahongida," in the *National Concord* (27 December 1987). Page 10 quotes these lines and says they are postulation of Odolaye Aremu which is now being confirmed in Obasanjo—*Nigerian Tribune* relationship which he describes as an "erstwhile deadly foe" of Obasanjo, is now one of his "ardent defenders."
22 Ibid., "Shehu Shangari Gemi Ijoba," ASCLP Q58A, 1979.
23 Personal interview with Jaigbade Alao, 9 August 1987. He chants the lines on the interview.
24 For information on these theories, see Chapter 2.
25 Ibid.
26 Ibid.
27 I attended many of the performances, and no one performance is identical (100%) to the other. In fact, all the Dàdàkúàdá artists interviewed expressed this fact.

Bibliography

Abimbola, Wande. *Yoruba Oral Tradition: Selections from the Papers Presented at the Seminar on Yoruba Oral Tradition: Poetry in Music, Dance, and Drama.* Ile-Ife, Nigeria: Dept. of African Languages and Literatures, U of Ife, 1975.

Achebe, Chinua. "The Use of African Literature," in *Okike: An African Journal of New Writing,* 16 (1979): 8–17.

Adéèkó, Adéléke. *Proverbs, Textuality, and Nativism in African Literature.* Gainesville: UP of Florida, 1998.

Ajayi, Y.A. "Asa: A public entertainment in Ilorin Area, Kwara State." M.A. Thesis, U of Ibadan, 1982.

Akínyemí, Akíntúndé. *Yorùbá Royal Poetry: A Socio-Historical Exposition and Annotated Translation.* Bayreuth: Bayreuth U, 2004.

Alao, Jaigbade. Ile Aliagan, Oloje Housing Estate, Ilorin. Personal interview, May, 2008.

———. Dàdàkúàdá artist, Ilorin. Ile Baba-Oyo, Ilorin. Personal interview, 9 August, 1987.

Alayande, Adebayo. Controller of Yoruba Program, Radio Kwara, Ilorin, Ilorin. Personal interview, 3 September, 1987.

Aliagan, Isiaka. *Oba Mama.* Ilorin: NNI Publishers Ltd., 2003.

Allison, Christine. *The Yezidi Oral Tradition in Iraqi Kurdistan.* London: Routledge, 2015.

Amao, E.O. "Baluu chnats and Songs in Ilorin, Kwara State." M.A. Thesis, U of Ibadan, 1983.

Amao, Omoekee, Dàdàkúàdá artist, Ilorin. Olelele, Ilorin. Personal interview, 8 August, 1987.

Anyidoho, Kofi. "Realism in Oral Narrative Performance," in *Acta Ethnographica Academiae Scientiarum Hungaricae,* 34.1–4 (1986–1988): 49–63.

———. "Mythmaker and Mythbreaker: The Oral Poet as Earwitness" in *African Literature in its Social and Political Dimensions.* Ed. Eileen Julien, Mortimer Mildred, and Curtis Schade. Washington: African Literature Association and Three Continents P, 1983, 5–14.

Arberry, Arthur J. *Arabic Poetry: A Primer for Students.* London: Cambridge UP, 1965.

Austen, Ralph A. (ed.) *In Search of Sunjata: The Mande Oral Epic as History, Literature, and Performance.* Bloomington: Indiana UP, 1999.

————. *The Elusive Epic: Performance, Text and History in the Oral Narrative of Jeki la Njambe (Cameroon Coast).* Atlanta: African Studies Association, 1995.

Babalola, A. "The Characteristic Feature of Outer Form of Yoruba Ijala Chants," in *Odu: Journal of African Studies*, 1.1 (1964): 39.

Bamgbose, A. *Yoruba Orthography.* Ibadan: Ibadan UP, 1965.

Bender, Mark. "Oral Performance and Orally Related Literature in China" in *Teaching Oral Traditions.* Ed. John Miles Foley. New York: Modern Language Association of America, 1998.

Berg, Hans C. ten. "Two Ways of Translating Oral Poetry," in *Dispositio: Revista Americana de Estudios Comparados Culturales/American Journal of Comparative and Cultural Studies*, 7.19–21 (1982): 239–47.

Bernardini, Wesley. *Hopi Oral Tradition and the Archeology of Identity.* Tucson, AZ: U of Arizona P, 2016.

Blakely, Pamela A. Reese. "Performing Dangerous Thoughts: Women's Song-Dance Performance Events in a Hemba Funeral Ritual (Republic of Zaire)." PhD Thesis, Indiana U, 1993.

Boadi, L.A. "Praise Poetry in Akan," in *Research in African Literatures*, 20.2 (Summer 1989): 181–93.

Bodunde, Charles. *Oral Traditions and Aesthetic Transfer: Form and Social Vision in Black Poetry.* Bayreuth: Bayreuth U, 2001

Bólájí, Emmanuel Bámidélé. "The Dynamics and the Manifestations of Efè: The Satirical Poetry of the Yoruba Gèlèdé Groups of Nigeria." PhD Thesis, U of Birmingham, 1984.

Bourke, Angela. "Performing, Not Writing: The Reception of an Irish Woman's Lament," in *Dwelling in Possibility: Women Poets and Critics on Poetry.* Ed. Yopie Prins and Maeera Shreiber. Ithaca, NY: Cornell UP, 1997, 132–46.

Brown, Duncan. *Oral Literature and Performance in South Africa.* Oxford: J Currey, 1999.

————. *Voicing the Text: South African Oral Poetry and Performance.* Cape Town; New York: Oxford UP, 1998.

Busby, Keith. "Mise en texte as Indicator of Oral Performance in Old French Verse Narrative," in *Performing Medieval Narrative.* Ed. Evelyn Birge Vitz, Regalado, Nancy Freeman, and Marilyn Lawrence. Cambridge, England: Brewer, 2005.

Camara, Seydou. "The Epic of Sunjata: Structure, Preservation, and Transmission," in *In Search of Sunjata: The Mande Oral Epic as History, Literature, and Performance.* Ed. Ralph A. Austen. Bloomington: Indiana UP; 1999.

Castro, Estelle. "Back and Forth… From Text to Performance: Open and Spoken Texts or the Practice of (Un)Writing in Aboriginal Poetry," in *Commonwealth Essays and Studies*, 28.1 (2005): 53–63.

Chidi, Amuta. *The Theory of African Literature.* London; New Jersey: Zed Books Ltd., 1989.

Chuckwuma, H.O. "The Oral Nature of Traditional Poetry and Language," in *Journal of the American Philosophical Association*, 82 (1976): 12–22.

Conteh-Morgan, John and Tejumola Olaniyan. *African Drama and Performance*. Bloomington: Indiana UP, 2004.

Courlander, Harold. *A Treasury of African Folklore: The Oral Literature, Traditions, Myths, Legends, Epics, Tales, Recollections, Wisdom, Sayings and Humor of Africa*. New York: Da Capo P; Marlowe & Co ed. Edition, 1995.

Daba, H.A. "The Case of Dan Maraya Jos: A Hausa Poet" in *Oral Poetry in Nigeria*. Ed. Uchegbulan N. Abalogu, G. Ashiwaju, and R. Amadi-Tshiwala. Lagos: Nigeria Magazine, 1981.

Dandatti, A. "The Role of an Oral Singer in Hausa-Fulani Society." Doctoral Dissertaion, Indiana U, 1975.

Danmole, Hakeem Olumide Akanni. "The Frontier Emirate: A History of Islam in Ilorin." PhD Thesis, U of Birmingham, Center of West African Studies, 1981.

Derico, T.M. *Oral Tradition and Synoptic Verbal Agreement: Evaluating the Empirical Evidence for Literary Dependence*. Eugene, OR: Pickwick Publications, 2016.

Dörnyei, Zoltán. "The Role of Individual and Social Variables in Oral Task Performance," in *Language Teaching Research*, 4.3 (2000): 275–300.

Doumeric, Eric. "Poetry and Orality," in *An Introduction to Poetry in English*. Ed. Eric Doumeric and Wendy Harding. Toulouse: PU du Mirail, 2007, 51–62.

Dube, Pamela Z. "We Have Something to Say for Ourselves! Contemporary First Nations Oral Performances," in *Zeitschrift für Kanada-Studien*, 16.1 [29] (1996): 139–47.

Duggan, Joseph J. "Chanson de Guillaume, 1. 103, Oral Composition and Textual Criticism," in *Olifant: A Publication of the Société Rencesvals*, 23.2 (2004): 9–24.

Evers, Larry and Barre Toelken (ed.). *Native American Oral Traditions: Collaboration and Interpretation*. Logan, UT: Utah State UP, 2001.

Echezona, W.W.C. "Ibo Musical Instrument in Ibo Culture." Doctoral Thesis, Michigan State U, 1963.

Falola, Toyin and Tyler Flaming (eds.). *Music, Performance, and African Identities*. New York: Routledge, 2012.

Farmer, Henry George. "The Music of Islam," in *The New Oxford History of Music* (London; New York: Oxford UP, 1965).

———. *Historical Facts for the Arabian Musical Influence*. London: The New Temple P, 1919.

Finnegan, R. *Oral Literature in Africa*. Oxford: Oxford UP, 1967.

Foley, John Miles. *How to Read an Oral Poem*. Urbana: U of Illinois P, 2002.

Frank, Roberta. "The Search for the Anglo-Saxon Oral Poet," in *Bulletin of the John Rylands University Library of Manchester*, 75.1 (1993): 11–36.

Franco, Mark (ed.) *Ritual and Event: Interdisciplinary Perspectives*. London: Routledge, 2007.

Friedman, Alan W. *Party Pieces: Oral Storytelling and Social Performance in Joyce and Beckett*. Syracuse, NY: Syracuse UP, 2007.

Gorlin, Dan. *Songs of West Africa: A Collection of Over 80 Traditional West African Folk Songs and Chants in 6 Languages with Translations,*

Annotations, and Performance notes. Forest Knolls, CA: Aloki West African Dance, 2000.

Gunner, Liz. "New African Oral Literatures," in *Revue de Litterature Comparee*, 67.1 (1993): 91–99.

Hagher, I. "Performance in TIV oral poetry," in *Oral Poetry in Nigeria.* Eds. U.N. Abalogu et al. Lagos: Nigerian Magazine, 1981.

Hale, Thomas A. *Griots and Griottes: Masters of Words and Music.* Bloomington: Indiana UP, 1998.

Hale, Thomas, Nouhou Malio, and Mounkaila Maiga. *The Epic of Askia Mohammed.* Bloomington: Indiana UP, 1996.

Harris, Joseph. *The Ballad and Oral Literature.* (Harvard English Studies), Cambridge, MA: Harvard UP, 1991.

Hermon-Hodge, H.B. *Gazetteer of Ilorin Province.* London: George Allen & Unwin Ltd., 1929.

Hess, Linda. *Bodies of Song: Kabir Oral Traditions and Performative Worlds in North India.* New York: Oxford UP, 2015.

Hiroaki, Yamashita. "The Japanese Tale of the Heike," in *Oral Tradition*, 18.1 (2003): 30–32.

Honko, Lauri. "The Quest for the Long Epic: Three Cases," in *Dynamics of Tradition: Perspectives on Oral Poetry and Folk Belief.* Ed. Lotte Tarkka. Helsinki: Finnish Literature Society, 2003.

———. "The Kalevala as Performance," in *The Kalevala and the World's Traditional Epics.* Ed. Lauri Honko. Helsinki: Finnish Literature Society, 2002, 485.

———. (ed.). *Textualization of Oral Epics.* Berlin: M. de Gruyter, 2000.

Imbo, Samuel Oluoch. *Oral Traditions as Philosophy: Okot p'Bitek's Legacy for African Philosophy.* Lanham, MD: Rowman & Littlefield Publishers, 2002.

Irele, Abiola. *African Imagination: Literature in Africa and the Black Diaspora.* Oxford: Oxford UP, 2001.

Johnson, John Williams, et al. *Oral Epics from Africa: Vibrant Voices from a Vast Continent.* Bloomington: Indiana UP, 1997.

Johnson, Samuel. *The History of the Yoruba.* Ed. O. Johnson. Lagos: CMS (Nigeria) Bookshop, 1969.

Joseph, A.A. "Towards a definition of Yoruba oral poetics." M.A. Thesis, U of Ibadan, 1986.

Kabira, Wanjiku Mukabi. *Gikuyu Oral Literature.* Nairobi: Heinemann Kenya, 1988.

Kolobo, Saka. Dàdàkúàdá artist, Ilorin. Adangba, Ilorin. Personal interview, June 2007.

———. Dàdàkúàdá artist, Ilorin. Adangba, Ilorin. Personal interview, 18 August, 1987.

Kurpershoek, P. Marcel. *Oral Poetry and Narratives from Central Arabia, I: The Poetry of ad-Dindan: A Bedouin Bard in Southern Najd.* Leiden: Brill, 1994.

Langellier, Kristin M. "From Text to Social Context," in *Literature in Performance: A Journal of Literary and Performing Art*, 6.2 (1986): 60–70.

Lasebikan, E.L. "The Tonal Structure of Yoruba Poetry," *Presence Africaine*, 1956, 43.

———. "Tone in Yoruba poetry," *Odu*, 2, 1955, 35–36.

Lee, Peter H. "From Oral to Written Literature," in *A History of Korean Literature*. Ed. Peter H. Lee. Cambridge, England: Cambridge UP, 2003, 52–65.

Leech, G.N. *A Linguistic Guide to English Poetry*. Harlow: Longman, 1969, 139.

Locke, David. *Kpegisu: A War Drum of the Ewe*. Tempe, AZ: White Cliffs Media Co.; 1992.

Lord, A.B. "Composition by Theme in Homer and South Slavic Epos," in *Transactions and Proceedings of the American Philological Association*, 82 (1951): 71–78.

Lowie, Robert H. *Myths and Traditions of the Crow Indians (Sources of American Indian Oral literature)*. Lincoln: U of Nebraska P, 1993.

Lukman, Habeebah. "Ere Olomooba." M.A. Thesis, U of Ilorin, 1996.

Mack, Douglas S. "James Hogg, Elizabeth Gaskell, and the Tradition of Oral Storytelling." in *Gaskell Society Journal*, 8 (1994): 70–76.

McAllister, P.A. *Xhosa Beer Drinking Rituals: Power, Practice and Performance in the South African Rural Periphery*. Durham: Carolina Academic P, 2006.

McBratney, John. India's 'Hundred Voices': Subaltern Oral Performance in Forster's a Passage to India," in *Oral Tradition*, 17.1 (2002): 108–34.

McGeachy, M.G. *Lonesome Words: The Vocal Poetics of the Old English Lament and the African-American Blues Song*. New York: Palgrave Macmillan, 2006.

McNaughton, Patrick R. *A Bird Dance Near Saturday City: Sidi Ballo and the Art of West African Masquerade*. Bloomington: Indiana UP, 2008.

Milubi, N.A. "Development of Venda Poetry from Oral Tradition to the Present Forms," in *South African Journal of African Languages/Suid-Afrikaanse Tydskrif vir Afrikatale*, 8.2 (1988): 56–60.

Miruka, Okumba. *Oral Literature of the Luo* (Vitabu Vya Sayari Series, 8) (English and Luo Edition). Nairobi: East African Educ. Publ., 2004.

Mulokozi, M.M. "The Nanga Epos of the Bahaya: A Case Study in African Epic Characteristics." Doctoral Thesis, U of Dar es Salaam, 1986.

Mustapha, Oyèbámijí. "A Literary Appraisal of Sákára: A Yoruba Traditional Form of Music," in *Yoruba Oral Tradition: Selections from the Papers Presented at the Seminar on Yoruba Oral Tradition: Poetry in Music, Dance and Drama*. Ile-Ife: Department of African Languages and Literatures, U of Ife, 1975, 517–49.

Mwangola, Mshai, "Transcending Boundaries: Performing the Contemporary African Diaspora." Presented in the IADDP Lecture Series, Western Ilinois U, 12 April, 2006.

Na'Allah, A. *Globalization, Oral Performance, and African Traditional Poetry*. New York; London: Palgrave Macmillan, 2018.

———. *African Discourse in Islam, Oral Traditions, and Performance*. New York: Routledge, 2010.

———. "Interpretation of African Orature: Oral Specificity and Literary Analysis," in *Alif: Journal of Comparative Poetics*, 17 (1997): 125–42.

———. "Oral and performatic arts of Ilorin," *The Herald*, 8 September, 1987.

———. "The Africanness of African poetry," *The Punch*, 7 February, 1987, 10.

———. "Arts and revolution in Africa," *The Punch*, 15 January, 1986, 9.

———. "Dàdàkúàdá: The Music of Ilorin," *Nigerian Herald*, 5 November, 1985, 6.

———. "Arabic and Islamic education in Ilorin," *Unilorin Pedagoque*, 1985, 37–50.

Nadel, S.F. *Nupe Religion*. London: Routledge; Kegan Paul Ltd., 1954.

Nagy, Falaky Joseph. "Models of Performance in Oral Epic, Ballad, and Song," *Western Folklore*, 62.1–2 (2003): 5–149.

Niles, John D. "The Myth of the Anglo-Saxon Oral Poet," *Western Folklore*, 62.1–2 (2003): 7–61.

Nixon, Robert. "Reception Theory and African Oral Literature: The Question of Performance," *English in Africa*, 12.2 (1985): 53–61.

Oboe, Annalisa. "The TRC Women's Hearings as Performance and Protest in the New South Africa," *Research in African Literatures*, 38.3 (2007): 60–76.

Odee, Saara. Housewife, Ile Ololu, Ita-Ogunbo, Ilorin. Ilorin. Personal interview, 2 September, 1987.

Ogede, Ode. *Art, Society and Performance: Igede Praise Poetry*. Gainesville: UP of Florida, 1997.

———. "The Power of Word in Igede Incantatory Poetry." *Africana Marburgensia*, 27.1–2. 1994, 13–20.

Ojaide, Tanure. *Theorizing African Oral Poetic Performance and Aesthetics: Udje Dance Songs of the Urhobo People*. Trenton, NJ: African World P, 2009.

Ojiaku, Ezike I.P.A. "Igbo Divination Poetry," in *Abu Afa: An Introduction*, 150 (1984): 37.

Okafor, C. "Research Methodology in African Oral Literature," in *Okike: An African Journal of New Writing*, 16 (1979): 83–97.

Okagbue, Osy A. *African Theatres and Performances*. London: Routledge, 2007.

Okoh, Nkem. "Bridges. Writing African Oral Literature: A Reading of Okot p'Bitek's Song of Lawino," in *Bridges: An African Journal of English Studies/Revue Africaine d'Etudes Anglaises*, 5.2 (1993): 35–53.

Okpewho, Isidore. "The Resources of the Oral Epic," in *African Intellectual Heritage*. Ed. Molefi Kete Asante and Abu S. Abarry. Philadelphia: Temple UP, 1996, 119–30.

———. *The Epic in Africa: Toward a Poetics of the Oral Performance*. New York: Columbia UP, 1979.

Okwori, Jenkeri. *Ije: The Performamce Traditions of the Idoma*. Zaria: Instances Communication Resource Centre, 1998.

Olátúnjí, Olátúndé O. "Characteristic Features of Yoruba Oral Poetry." Doctoral Thesis, U of Ibadan, 1970.

Olajubu, I.O. "Iwi: Egungun Chants in Yoruba Oral Literature." M.A. Thesis, U of Lagos, 1970.

Olaoye, R.A. "The Ilorin Emirate and the British Ascedency 1897–1918: An Overview of the Early Phase of Ilorin Provincial Administration." M.A. Thesis, U of Ilorin, 1984.

Oloje, Lanrewaju. Dàdàkúàdá Artist, Ilorin. Oloje, Ilorin. Personal interview, June 2007.

———. Dàdàkúàdá Artist, Ilorin. Oloje, Ilorin. Personal interview, 28 August, 1987.

Oloru, AbdulRasaq Jimoh. *A Guide to Ilorin*. Ilorin: Famost (Nig.) Limited, 1998.

Omoniwa, Olarewaju. "The Performance Context and Career of Ijumu Hunter-Poet," in *Nigerian Heritage: Journal of the National Commission for Museums and Monuments*, 6 (1997): 11–20.

Onabiyi-Obidike, M.A. "Islam Influence on Yoruba Music," in *African Notes*, 8.2 (1981): 37–51.

Opland, Jeff. "Praise Poetry: Praise Poetry of the Xhosa," in *African Folklore: An Encyclopedia*. New York: Routledge, 2004, 361–62.

———. "The Making of a Xhosa Oral Poem," in *De Gustibus: Essays for Alain Renoir*. Ed. John Miles Foley et al. New York: Garland, 1992, 411–40.

———. "The Bones of Mfanta: A Xhosa Oral Poet's Response to Context in South Africa," in *Research in African Literatures*, 18.1 (1987): 36–50.

Opler, Morris E. and Scott Rushforth. *Myths and Tales of the Chiricahua Apache Indians (Sources of American Indian Oral Literature)*. Lincoln: U of Nebraska, 1994.

Ose, Aremu. Dàdàkúàdá artist, Ilorin. Amule, Ilorin. Personal interview, 26 August, 1987.

Osundare, Niyi. "Poems for Sale: Stylistic Features of Yoruba Ipolowo Poetry," in *African Notes*, 15.1, 2 (1991): 63–92.

Parry, Nilman. "Studies in the Epic Technique of Oral Verse-Making I: The Homeric Language as Languages of an Oral Poet," in *Harvard Studies in Classical Philosophy*, 41 (1930): 73–147.

Ravelhofer, Barbara. "Oral Poetry and the Printing Press in Byron's The Giaour (1813)," in *Romanticism: The Journal of Romantic Culture and Criticism*, 11.1 (2005): 23–40.

Reichl, Karl. "Oral Tradition and Performance of the Uzbek and Karakalpak Epic Singers" in *Fragen der mongolischen Heldendichtung, III*. Ed. Walther Heissig. Wiesbaden: Harrassowitz, 1985.

Rowbottom, Anne. "The Real Royalists': Folk Performance and the Civil Religion at Royal Visits," *Folklore*, 109 (1998): 77–88.

Roy, Christopher D. *African Art as Theatre [videorecording]: The Bwa Masks of the Gnou mou family of the village of Boni*. Laughing Films and the Art and Life in African Project Present. United States, 2006.

Sawyer, R. Keith. "The Semiotics of Improvisation: The Pragmatics of Musical and Verbal Performance," in *Semiotica: Journal of the International Association for Semiotic Studies/Revue de l'Association Internationale*, 108.3–4 (1996): 269–306.

Scheub, Harold. "Oral Poetry and History," in *New Literary History: A Journal of Theory and Interpretation*, 18.3 (1987): 477–96.

Sietsema, B. "Stress and Tone in Yoruba World Composition," in *Linqua*, 8.4 (1959): 385–402.

Smith, Diana. *Performing Literature: Oral Interpretation & Drama Studies for Christian Schools*. Greenville, SC: Bob Jones UP, 2002.

Stanley, M. "African Aesthetics in Traditional African Art," in *Okeke: An African Journal of New Writing*. New York: NOK Publishers Ltd., 5, 1974, 13–24.

Steinmeyer, Elke. "Chanting the Song of Sorrow: Threnody in Homer and Zakes Mda," *Current Writing: Text and Reception in Southern Africa*, 15.2 (2003): 156–72.

Ugoretz, Joseph. "The Pitchman in Print: Oral Performance Art in Text and Context." Doctoral Dissertation, City U of New York, 2000.

Vansina, Jan and H.M. Wright. *Oral Tradition: A Study in Historical Methodology*. Chicago, IL: Aldine Transaction, 2006.

Von Geldern, James. "The Ode as a Performative Genre" in *Slavic Review: American Quarterly of Russian, Eurasian and East European Studies*, 50.4 (1991): 927–39.

Waterman, Christopher Alan. *Juju: A Social History and Ethnography of an African Popular Music*. Chicago, IL: U of Chicago P, 1990.

Warren, Liz. *The Oral Tradition Today: An Introduction to the Art of Storytelling*. New York: Pearson Learning Solutions, 2008.

Wilks, "Ivor. The History of the Sunjata Epic: A Review of the Evidence," in *Search of Sunjata: The Mande Oral Epic as History, Literature, and Performance*. Ed. Ralph A. Austen. Bloomington: Indiana UP, 1999.

Wood, Brent. "Robert Hunter's Oral Poetry: Mind, Metaphor, and Community," *Poetics Today*, 24.1 (2003): 35–63.

Yai, Olabiyi. Yai, Olabiyi Babalola. "Tradition and the Yoruba Artist," in *African Arts*, 32.1 (1999): 32–35.

———. "Issues in Oral Poetry: Criticism, Teaching, and Translation," in *Georgetown University Round Table on Languages and Linguistics* (1987): 91–106.

Index

Taylor & Francis Group
an **informa** business

Taylor & Francis eBooks

www.taylorfrancis.com

A single destination for eBooks from Taylor & Francis
with increased functionality and an improved user
experience to meet the needs of our customers.

90,000+ eBooks of award-winning academic content in
Humanities, Social Science, Science, Technology, Engineering,
and Medical written by a global network of editors and authors.

TAYLOR & FRANCIS EBOOKS OFFERS:

A streamlined
experience for
our library
customers

A single point
of discovery
for all of our
eBook content

Improved
search and
discovery of
content at both
book and
chapter level

REQUEST A FREE TRIAL
support@taylorfrancis.com

Routledge
Taylor & Francis Group

CRC Press
Taylor & Francis Group

For Product Safety Concerns and Information please contact our EU
representative GPSR@taylorandfrancis.com
Taylor & Francis Verlag GmbH, Kaufingerstraße 24, 80331 München, Germany

www.ingramcontent.com/pod-product-compliance
Lightning Source LLC
Chambersburg PA
CBHW050526270326
41926CB00015B/3090